HITCHCOCK ANNUAL
2023

T0355391

ANNUAL *Hitchcock*

27

———— 2023 ————

Editor
Sidney Gottlieb

Editorial Advisory Board
Richard Allen   Thomas L. Leitch
James Naremore   David Sterritt

Founding Editor
Christopher Brookhouse

Editorial Associate
Renata Jackson

Cover Design
Deborah Dutko

We evaluate manuscripts for the *Hitchcock Annual* throughout the year. Send any correspondence by mail to Sidney Gottlieb, Department of Communication and Media Studies, Sacred Heart University, 5151 Park Avenue, Fairfield, Connecticut 06825. Send submissions by e-mail to spgottlieb@aol.com

We invite articles on all aspects of Hitchcock's life, works, and influence, and encourage a variety of critical approaches, methods, and viewpoints. For all submissions, follow the guidelines of the *Chicago Manual of Style*, using full notes rather than works cited format. We prefer submissions by e-mail, in any standard word processing format, which makes it easier to circulate essays for editorial review. The responsibility for securing any permissions required for publishing material in the essay rests with the author. Illustrations may be included, but as separate JPG or TIF files rather than as part of the text file. Decision time is normally within three months. The submission of an essay indicates your commitment to publish it, if accepted, in the *Hitchcock Annual*, and that it is not simultaneously under consideration for publication elsewhere.

For all orders, including back issues, contact Columbia University Press, 61 West 62nd Street, New York, NY 10023; www.columbia/edu/cu/cup

The *Hitchcock Annual* is indexed in the *Film Literature Index* and *MLA International Bibliography*.

♕ Columbia University Press   *New York*

Columbia University Press
Publishers Since 1893
New York   Chichester, West Sussex

ISBN 978-0-231-21697-5 (pbk.)
ISSN 1062-5518

Thomas Leitch

The Whole Hitchcock, and Nothing But the Parts

Hitchcock's Detractors Miss the Point

Over his fifty-year directorial career, Alfred Hitchcock attracted many dismissive responses that have been largely forgotten in the course of his ascension into the cinematic pantheon. One of the most striking of these attacks is Graham Greene's 1936 review of *Secret Agent*:

> How unfortunate it is that Mr. Hitchcock, a clever director, is allowed to produce and even to write his own films, though as a producer he has no sense of continuity and as a writer he has no sense of life. His films consist of a series of small "amusing" melodramatic situations. . . . Very perfunctorily he builds up to these tricky situations (paying no attention on the way to inconsistencies, loose ends, psychological absurdities) and then drops them: they mean nothing: they lead to nothing.[1]

Thirty-six years later, Greene doubled down on this assessment. His 1972 introduction to his collected film reviews makes it clear that "Hitchcock's 'inadequate sense of reality,'" presumably arising from his having no sense of continuity and no sense of life, which also "spoilt *The Thirty-Nine Steps*," continued to irritate him over thirty years later despite François Truffaut's full-throated defense of Hitchcock, which he cites only to dismiss in turn.[2]

Although Greene famously called his own most popular novels, from *Orient Express* (1932) to *Our Man in Havana* (1958), "entertainment[s]" that lacked the thematic gravitas that would allow them to stand as equals alongside weightier novels like *The Power and the Glory* (1940) and *The Comedians* (1966), his complaint is not that Hitchcock's films are frivolous melodramas, for he acknowledges that "I have always enjoyed reading melodrama, and I enjoy writing it," but that they are not successful melodramas.[3] Even so, it is tempting to react to his dismissal by saying that Greene has missed the whole point of Hitchcock's films, just as Robin Wood argued a generation later that Penelope Houston missed the whole point of *The Birds* (1963) when she announced that Hitchcock "scared us in *Psycho* enough to makes us think twice about stopping at any building remotely resembling the Bates Motel. He tries it again in *The Birds*, but we will happily go on throwing bread to the seagulls, because the film can't for long enough at a time break through our barrier of disbelief."[4] Early and late in his career, a significant number of detractors, denigrating Hitchcock's intermittent mastery of larger narrative arcs, either overlooked the fact that he sometimes cared more for individual moments than larger structures or attacked him for that preference.

Whether his focus is on individual moments or larger structures, the stories Hitchcock tells are primarily a means to the end of manipulating his audience. What I have called his "ludic approach to storytelling" constantly plays games with, and sometimes against, his audience, using movies as his medium or playing field.[5] That is why Hitchcock routinely shows such contempt for what he calls "the plausibles," and why his interest in character as such is so often limited, as the frustration of so many of his performers seeking direction have attested.[6] His fundamental approach to storytelling is so frequently focused on the set pieces Greene hated that his relative neglect of these other factors is a feature, not a bug. So the standards by which Greene is judging Hitchcock might be characterized as irrelevant as they would be to board games like Monopoly or video games like Tetris.

That is not to say that Greene was immune to Hitchcock's appeal. His much more sympathetic review of *Sabotage* (1937)

Calaveras that same year by combining reshot versions of the same two short films, clearly thought that keeping Laurel and Hardy's audience laughing was more important than maintaining the narrative integrity of those original shorts.

An even more obvious example is pornography, which no one watches for the story—though that proposition is complicated for me by a pair of episodes from my time in graduate school. The first of these involved two young women who sat behind me at a screening of Just Jaeckin's soft-core classic *Emmanuele* (1974) whispering excitedly to each other during the first fifteen minutes about how beautiful the heroine's clothes were and what a great house she lived in. Clearly their ideas about the film's most memorable attractions, and their willingness to immerse themselves in a larger narrative, were different from mine. A year or so later, on a day that I felt the need for a break from reading *King Lear*, I phoned my local adult cinema to ascertain the starting times for the two features it was showing. After a long pause, the employee who answered the phone told me, "You can arrive at any time, sir. We have what you're looking for." She provided a salutary reminder of something I had forgotten: that nearly everyone watches porn for the good parts, not for the story.

Audiences watch many other kinds of movies for the good parts. The publicity tag for J. Lee Thompson's *Happy Birthday to Me* (1981), "Six of the most bizarre murders you will ever see," suggests that the target audience for many horror films is less interested in the overarching narrative than in a series of gruesome and inventive set pieces. This emphasis on striking parts over formulaic wholes has encouraged enterprising producers to create and extend evergreen horror franchises like *The Texas Chainsaw Massacre* (nine films, 1974–2022), *Halloween* (thirteen films, 1978–2022), *Friday the 13th* (twelve films, 1980–2009), *A Nightmare on Elm Street* (nine films, 1984–2010), and *Saw* (ten films, 2004–24, with an eleventh due for release in 2025). One reason the films in the *Saw* franchise, along with the three films in the *Hostel* franchise (2006–11), are often labeled "horror porn" is that audiences are assumed to be watching them primarily for the good parts.

The cinema of attractions has survived in many genres that are rarely compared to pornography. Disaster movies of the 1970s like Ronald Neame's *The Poseidon Adventure* (1972), Mark Robson's *Earthquake* (1974), and John Guillermin's *The Towering Inferno* (1974) present their larger conflicts through a series of thrilling individual scenes. The action franchises inspired in large part by disaster movies from John McTiernan's *Die Hard* (1988) to the James Bond movies feature set pieces that float increasingly free of their nominal sources by Ian Fleming and others. The closely related comic-book franchises about the D.C. and Marvel Universes continue to take their cue from what Gunning has called "the Lucas–Spielberg–Coppola cinema of effects."[13]

A more illustrious predecessor to the cinema of attractions that Gunning does not consider is grand opera, which contextualizes ritualistic and often familiar stories structurally by foregrounding arias, ensembles, and set pieces, and performatively by foregrounding beloved or promising stars. No one would argue that every aria in *Aida* has been written primarily to advance the story; it is at least equally true that the story has been shaped specifically to showcase these set pieces, whose dramatic and performative force are related but distinct. The distinctive attractions of the form make it hard to imagine an opera buff declining an invitation to *Don Giovanni* or *La Bohème* by saying, "Oh, no, thanks. I already know the story."

One final example of the cinema of attractions particularly relevant to Hitchcock is detective stories—not films based on the Golden Age whodunits of Agatha Christie, but those based on the private eye stories whose structure their first and most influential theorist, Raymond Chandler, memorably described by contrasting the new formula with the old:

> The emotional basis of the standard detective story was and had always been that murder will out and justice will be done. Its technical basis was the relative insignificance of everything except the final denouement. What led up to that was more or less

passage-work. The denouement would justify everything. The technical basis of the *Black Mask* type of story on the other hand was that the scene outranked the plot, in the sense that a good plot was one which made good scenes. The ideal mystery was one you would read if the end was missing. We who tried to write it had the same point of view as the film makers. When I first went to work in Hollywood a very intelligent producer told me that you couldn't make a successful motion picture from a mystery story, because the whole point was a disclosure that took a few seconds of screen time when the audience was reaching for its hat. He was wrong, but only because he was thinking of the wrong kind of mystery.[14]

Chandler's assumption that the final destination of a mystery is less important than the journey to that destination is abundantly supported by his own practice. For like those early foreign-language feature films of Laurel and Hardy, three of Chandler's first four novels were cobbled together—cannibalized, as Chandler put it—from short stories he had published years before. Even more noteworthy than the questionable ethics of this self-cannibalization is its very possibility. *The Big Sleep* (1939), *Farewell, My Lovely* (1940), and *The Lady in the Lake* (1944) all come across as cluttered but perfectly acceptable adventures for Philip Marlowe, partly because Chandler's stories are so formulaic in their character types and incidents that they can be dovetailed together without any obvious sense of incongruity, partly because he places so much more emphasis on compelling scenes than compelling plots.

Hitchcock's Champions Miss the Point

As his fame grew, Hitchcock's detractors increasingly became a minority party, and their complaints about his attraction to attractions came to seem more marginal and cantankerous. At the same time, the early critics who sought to rescue Hitchcock from his detractors by emphasizing his mastery of narrative form, thematic subtlety, and complex relationships with his audience that required significant amounts of time to develop, missed another, equally important point: Hitchcock never relinquished his attachment to isolated images, passing moments, and thrilling individual set pieces. Especially within the founding generation of Hitchcock scholarship, the director's champions, whatever their differences, all agreed that the principal value of Hitchcock's attractions was the larger patterns they generated.

Writing a year before the release of *Vertigo* (1958), Eric Rohmer and Claude Chabrol began their pioneering study of Hitchcock by revealing the unifying figure they had found in Hitchcock's carpet:

> The idea of the "exchange," which we find everywhere in his work, may be given either a moral expression (the transfer of guilt), a psychological expression (suspicion), a dramatic expression (blackmail—or even more pure "suspense"), or a concrete expression (a to-and-fro movement).[15]

For Rohmer and Chabrol, the pattern of the exchange linked films as different as *Strangers on a Train* (1951), which revolves around a transfer of guilt; *Suspicion* (1941), which is driven by its heroine's slowly growing apprehension that her husband wants to kill her; *Blackmail* (1929), whose heroine is tormented by the fear that her killing of her would-be rapist will be exposed by a witness; and *Rear Window* (1954), which moves visually back and forth between its hero's apartment and the neighbors he spies on. But the exchange does not merely link these films: in serving as the "matrix-idea of the Hitchcockian system," it provides "the sense of a Unity which is the Unity of the world itself." In concluding that "in Hitchcock's work form does not embellish content, it creates it," Rohmer and Chabrol are not only subordinating the parts of Hitchcock's films to the larger forms of those films; they are reading each of the films as a part to be subordinated to the larger pattern of the director's career as a whole.[16]

Eight years later, in the first significant monograph on Hitchcock in English, Robin Wood sought to answer his leading question "Why should we take Hitchcock seriously?" by explicitly rejecting Hitchcock's own comments on his films. For Wood, "the chief obstacle in the way of a serious appraisal of Hitchcock's work for many people is Hitchcock's own attitude toward it," which he dismisses as "irrelevant." In Wood's analysis, the whole not only drives but redeems the parts. Wood is keenly interested in specific moments in the films, like the moment in *Marnie* (1964), when Marnie Edgar (Tippi Hedren) enters the house of her husband Mark Rutland (Sean Connery) after shooting her beloved horse Forio moments after Sidney Strutt (Martin Gabel), whom Mark is trying to prevent from prosecuting his wife for theft, venomously tells Mark, "Just wait till *you've* been victimized," and the moment when the camera watches from overhead as Norman Bates (Anthony Perkins) carries his mother out of her bedroom down to the fruit cellar in *Psycho* (1960). But he consistently uses these moments to demonstrate Hitchcock's "realization of theme in terms of 'pure cinema.'" Its thematic coherence is what makes *North by Northwest*, which "has a subject as well as a plot," so clearly superior to *Goldfinger* (1964), which despite borrowing much of Hitchcock's geographical sweep and seriocomic tone is merely "a collection of bits." It is not enough for *The Birds* to be a movie about increasingly large and menacing flocks of birds attacking human beings; there must be a reason for the attacks, and after considering several other possible reasons, Wood announces that the birds are "a concrete embodiment of the arbitrary and unpredictable . . . of the possibility that life is meaningless and absurd." Not surprisingly, Wood finds that "kisses in Hitchcock . . . are often used to reveal or epitomize a whole relationship and (if one works outward from that) the sense of a whole film."[17] Wood departs from Rohmer and Chabrol in focusing on Hitchcock's most notable films as individual achievements rather than chapters in a master text but retains their tendency to subordinate the parts of every film to the revelatory structure of the whole film. So every moment in Hitchcock becomes for Wood a synecdoche that is valuable precisely for what it reveals about the film's larger thematic patterns.

Writing in 1982, toward the end of this first generation of Hitchcock scholarship, William Rothman takes pains to distance himself from cinema studies' "all but unquestioned doctrine . . . that movies were pernicious ideological representations to be resisted and decoded, not treated with the respect due works of art capable of instructing us how to think about them."[18] Flying in the face of this theoretical hegemony, Rothman provides a meticulous, shot-by-shot analysis of five films from *The Lodger* to *Psycho* that focuses on much smaller moments and structures, most notably the four parallel vertical lines that he calls

> Hitchcock's //// motif. It recurs at significant junctures in every one of his films. At one level, the //// serves as a Hitchcock signature: it is his mark on the frame, akin to his ritual cameo appearances. At another level, it signifies the confinement of the camera's subject within the frame and within the world of the film. Like the profile shot, it announces that we have arrived at a limit of our access to the camera's subject; we might say that it stands for the barrier of the screen itself. It is also associated with sexual fear and the specific threat of loss of control or breakdown.[19]

Rothman's search for motivic patterns like //// is less invested in the larger narrative arc of any particular film than in what Fredric Jameson, in reviewing Rothman's *Hitchcock—The Murderous Gaze*, identified as "what it can tell us about *interpretation* as such, its conditions of possibility, what must be left out in order to include what it finally does manage to include."[20] The moral that Rothman extracts from *Psycho*—that "we have been born into the world and we are fated to die"— is one that he finds "at the heart of every film," for "if every authentic work of art bears a murderous aspect and calls for its creator's death and allows his rebirth, these conditions . . . are intrinsic to the very medium of film."[21] If Wood sees every detail in every Hitchcock film as a key to that film's unity, and Rohmer and Chabrol see every leading pattern in each of his films as a key to his career's unity, Rothman sees every moment in every Hitchcock film as key to the experience of lived mortality that the cinematic medium offers.

Whatever theories of Hitchcock, suspense, motion pictures, storytelling, or signification they espouse, the practice of more recent Hitchcock scholars is far more likely than that of Hitchcock's early champions to challenge the hierarchy of whole and parts. Matthew Bilodeau's 2022 online essay "Alfred Hitchcock Couldn't Have Cared Less About His Movies Making Sense," for example, quotes Hitchcock's interview with Truffaut repeatedly in support of the argument expressed by its title.[22] So it seems less tendentious now than it once did to claim, as I did some twenty-five years ago, that "Hitchcock's is preeminently a cinema of moments."[23] Many audiences, whatever their official positions on parts and wholes, continue to experience movies as collections of memorable performances, ideas, incidents, and spectacles whose whole is often much less important than the sum of their parts. Even Syd Field acknowledges that "Good scenes make good movies. When you think of a good movie, you remember *scenes*, not the entire film."[24]

Hitchcock's films, as countless interviews with his screenwriters have attested, were constructed not top-down, from compelling stories that generated interesting scenes, but bottom-up, as collections of scenes motivated by a single compelling narrative premise (a man suspected of murder is pursued by both the police and the actual criminals; a pair of killers invite the family and friends of their victim to a party at which the food is placed atop a chest containing the dead body; birds attack the residents of a California town for no discernible reason) or, more radically, collections of scenes he really wanted to film, integrated more or less successfully into a larger structure that emerged from them. It is true that Hitchcock's record, especially in his silent films, is often hit-and-miss. His most obvious miss, as he acknowledged himself, was *Champagne* (1928), which very few people outside Hitchcock circles have seen because it is such a forgettable film. *Champagne* can be profitably set against *Number Seventeen* (1932), which becomes a much more interesting and coherent film if it is approached as a series of games Hitchcock is using the characters to play with the audience. The setup is creaky, the characters are paper-thin, their motivations are utterly unrealistic, and the logic that holds the story together gets more and more preposterous as the film goes along—but none of that stops the film from being highly amusing from moment to moment, the goal Hitchcock is aiming for.

The Point of Integrating Parts into Wholes

Even in his maturity, Hitchcock's infatuation with attractions makes some of his films more successful than others, mainly because the attractions he loves to show off are more successfully integrated into a larger narrative arc to which he continues to profess indifference. Consider the increasing integration of his most show-offy productions, his four one-set films, in which the challenge of shooting a film on a single location poses a significant attraction to those in the know.

The camera setups in *Lifeboat* (1944) are basically a functional gimmick the film could easily have dispensed with. The fact that all but a handful of these setups are aboard the lifeboat manages to pull off the trick of creating a claustrophobic space in the middle of an otherwise deserted ocean. But the camerawork does so little to intensify the story that many audiences do not even notice the setups unless they are alerted to them in advance. Whether they like *Lifeboat* or not has very little to do with how impressed they are by the dexterity of the camera setups. Most of these can pass unnoticed because they are obvious—where else would you put the camera if you were filming a story about survivors of shipwreck in a lifeboat adrift on the Atlantic?—and making a point of noticing them might well distract audiences from the film's story instead of intensifying their attachment to it.

The apparently single-take *Rope* (1948) is equally gimmicky. But now the gimmick is far more relevant to both the source material, Patrick Hamilton's one-set 1929 play *Rope's End*, and the film's thematic and phenomenological goal of entrapping its audience by entrapping its characters in a single claustrophobic set. Even audience members who fail to notice that the film has been shot in a series of long takes—and I can attest from my years teaching the film that there are a surprising number of such filmgoers out there—still feel and respond to the more thematically driven sense of claustrophobia its camerawork engenders.

Dial M for Murder (1953), based on another one-set play, this time by Frederick Knott, feels less gimmicky and more naturalistic than *Rope*. In flat prints, *Dial M for Murder* is continuously entertaining, though in ways that depend more on its dialogue and its performances than on the relatively subtle camerawork that displays them. When audiences watch it in 3-D, as it was originally shot, it comes alive as much more subtly original in its subordination of the disruptive three-dimensional actions that dominate other 3-D films like Anthony C. Ferrante's *Sharknado* (2013), James Cameron's *Avatar* (2009), and even George Sidney's contemporaneous *Kiss Me Kate* (1953) to the surprisingly three-dimensional spaces in which the decorously murderous plot plays out.

But the most successful of these one-set films by far is *Rear Window*. One widely noted reason why is that its space is so much more complex and generously conceived, including the single room inside the Greenwich Village apartment of L.B. Jefferies (James Stewart), the interior courtyard several floors below, and the windows and fire escapes of half a dozen apartments in neighboring buildings, that some audiences do not consider it a one-set film at all. The film's visual imperative, which limits all but a dozen camera setups in the film's climactic sequence to spaces inside Jefferies's apartment, emphasizes both the powers and the limits of its photographer hero's point of view as he passes judgment on his neighbors without realizing for most of the film's running time that he would be equally subject to the judgment of any neighbors who happened to return his gaze. The film's screenplay is particularly attentive to the different ways the characters and subplots that play out before Jefferies's eyes can be integrated, not into the film's larger story, but into its larger thematic pattern of the vicissitudes of romantic love.

Turning from Hitchcock's one-set films to his man-on-the-run films makes it clear why *The 39 Steps* (1935), despite Graham Greene's objections, is still highly regarded after all these years. The nature of the film's success is brought into sharper relief by comparing its witty dialogue, its whirlwind pace, its deftly understated handling of the growing relationship between its hero and heroine, and its abrupt changes of tone from scene to scene, and sometimes within a scene, to the corresponding features of two other stories. One is the 1915 John Buchan novel the film adapts, which confronts Richard Hannay, a fugitive suspected of the murder of a visitor to his London flat, with an extravagant range of fanciful adventures ("The Adventure of the Literary Innkeeper," "The Adventure of the Radical Candidate," and others) presented in a sequence that could easily have been rearranged in any number of other permutations.[25]

By contrast, Hitchcock's film methodically dispatches the fleeing Hannay (Robert Donat) to Scotland, then intensifies his peril through the realization that the man he hoped would rescue him is in league with the spies from whom he is fleeing, and then brings him into collision with Pamela (Madeleine Carroll) who, along with Annabella Smith (Lucie Mannheim) and the crofter's wife (Peggy Ashcroft), is one of three new female characters the film introduces at pivotal moments, as the film hurtles toward its end. The other is *Saboteur* (1942), which follows Greene's strictures more closely because its hero's cross-country tour of the United States in pursuit of its eponymous villain is much more deliberate in its logic and pacing. But no one thinks *Saboteur* is as successful as *The 39 Steps*—not even Hitchcock, who confessed to Truffaut that it was cluttered with too many ideas; there's the hero in handcuffs leaping down from a bridge; the scene of the elderly blind man in the house; the ghost town with the deserted workyards; and the long shot of Boulder Dam. I think we covered too much ground. . . . The script lacks discipline. I don't think I exercised a clear, sharp approach to the original construction of the screenplay. There was a mass of ideas, but they weren't sorted out in proper order; they weren't selected with sufficient care. I feel the whole thing should have been pruned and tightly edited long before the actual shooting. It goes to show that a mass of ideas, however good they are, is not sufficient to create a successful picture. They've got to be carefully presented with a constant awareness of the shape of the whole.[26]

This post-mortem, which sounds like no one so much as Graham Greene, manages to combine two apparently irreconcilable tendencies in Hitchcock: the persistence throughout his career of a bottom-up approach to storytelling in which the whole grows out of the parts, not vice-versa, and an acknowledgment that successful wholes really are more than the sum of their parts.

Hitchcock Misses the Point

Although Hitchcock never made a private-eye film, he could well have been that very intelligent producer who told Raymond Chandler that you couldn't make a successful film from a mystery story. After all, he told Truffaut of *Murder!* (1930):

That was one of the rare whodunits I made. I generally avoid this genre because as a rule all of the interest is concentrated in the ending. . . . I don't really approve of whodunits because they're rather like a jigsaw or a crossword puzzle. No emotion. You simply wait to find out who committed the murder.[27]

Earlier in that same interview, Hitchcock expressed his strong preference for the "fifteen minutes of *suspense*" he could provide audiences by showing them a bomb hidden beneath a table to the "fifteen seconds of *surprise* at the moment of the explosion" if they did not already know about the bomb.[28]

Indeed Chandler's remarks about filming detective stories presage Hitchcock's own pronouncements about his relative indifference to the denouements of screen whodunits so precisely that it is tempting to ignore his influential champions and label Hitchcock, like Chandler, as a storyteller consistently more interested in parts than wholes. Hitchcock often seems to do everything he can to foster this impression himself. His book-length interview with Truffaut is studded with examples of shots he especially treasures in his own films. He sketches out the design for a shot in the opening sequence of *The Lodger* (1926) in which a police van seen from the rear was intended to give audiences "the impression of a face with two eyes and the eyeballs moving." He concludes his discussion of *Suspicion* by pointing out that he "put a light right inside the glass [of milk Johnnie Aysgarth (Cary Grant) is carrying up the stairs to the wife who thinks he wants to kill her] because I wanted it to be luminous." He pauses to describe in detail "an interesting shot in the courtroom when Louis Jourdan is called in to give evidence" in *The Paradine Case* (1947). When Truffaut notes appreciatively that in a ground-level shot of the railroad tracks in the opening of *Strangers on a Train*, "the separating rails suggest the idea of divergent courses—two different ways of life," Hitchcock pulls back from this thematic generalization to an aesthetic contemplation of the single shot: "Naturally, there is that as well. Isn't it a fascinating design? One could study it forever."[29]

But the situation is more complicated in ways that Hitchcock's repeated focus on small-scale effects in the Truffaut interview and elsewhere tends to overlook. Hitchcock's films do indeed represent an unusually compelling latter-day version of the cinema of attractions, marked in another way Gunning notes in a passage that ostensibly has nothing to do with Hitchcock: "The cinema of attractions expends little energy creating characters with psychological motivations or individual personality. . . . Its energy moves [outward] towards an acknowledged spectator rather than inward towards the character-based situations essential to classical narrative."[30] That is why, when Truffaut asked him, "Do you prefer to shoot a screenplay with strong situations and sketchy characters, or the opposite?" Hitchcock replied, "I prefer the strong situations. It is easier to put them into images. In order to probe a character in depth, you often need too many words."[31]

The director's well-documented preference for images over words routinely led him to gloss over the indispensable contributions of screenwriters like Eliot Stannard, whose name he never saw fit to mention in the book-length Truffaut interview even though Stannard wrote or co-wrote the screenplays for seven of the first nine films Hitchcock directed. Hitchcock's widely noted preference for paring back dialogue in so many of his films is linked to an even more pervasive blind spot that has been less often remarked upon: his insistence that individual visual effects are more important to his films than the kinds of larger narrative arcs that rely on dialogue.

Aristotle Misses the Point

The diffidence about both character and larger narrative structures that Hitchcock often expressed to interviewers taps into a much older narrative tradition that Hitchcock repeatedly espouses even though he shows no awareness of its antecedents. Contemporary filmgoers are most likely to have encountered this tradition in Aristotle's *Poetics*, which forcefully argues against it. After defining tragedy as "an imitation of an action" in Chapter 6 of the *Poetics*, Aristotle identifies the six indispensable elements of tragedy—"Plot, Character, Diction, Thought, Spectacle, Song"—and then defends the proposition that action is the most important of them:

Tragedy is an imitation not of men, but of action and of life, and life consists in action, and its end is a mode of action, not a quality. Now character determines men's qualities, but it is by their actions that they are happy or the reverse. Dramatic action, therefore, is not with a view to the representation of character: character comes in as subsidiary to the actions. . . . If you string together a set of speeches expressive of character, and well finished in point of diction and thought, you will not produce the essential tragic effect nearly so well as with a play which, however deficient in these respects, has a plot and artistically constructed incidents.[32]

Centuries of exposure to the *Poetics* have made passages like this sound as self-evident as Syd Field's remarks about the subordination of scenes to the stories they advance—of course plot is more important to tragedy than character, diction, or spectacle—but Aristotle himself clearly does not think his argument is self-evident, for in returning to it a few chapters later, he calls out errant tragedians:

Unity of plot does not, as some persons think, consist in the unity of the hero. For infinitely various are the incidents in one man's life which cannot be reduced to unity; and so, too, there are many actions of one man out of which we cannot make one action. Hence the error, as it appears, of all poets who have composed a Heracleid, or other poems of the kind. They imagine that as Heracles was one man, the story of Heracles must also be a unity.[33]

These references to what "some persons think" and to all those poets who have composed Heracleids indicate that Aristotle's definition of tragedy as the imitation of an action is offered specifically as a corrective to structural practices— building a tragedy out of a series of relatively unrelated incidents, or assuming that the adventures of a single hero amount to a coherent narrative—that Aristotle considers as widespread as they are misbegotten.

Despite Aristotle's briskly decisive intervention in the debate about the relative value of parts and wholes in tragedy, more general questions about what relations the parts of an entity have to the entity as such, and whether wholes should be defined as collections of parts or entities with their own distinctive identities, have provoked many debates in metaphysical and ontological theories that later theorists have proposed. So persistent have these debates been, in fact, in discussions from Plato's *Theaetetus* to Edmund Husserl's *Logical Investigations*, that philosophers have placed them in their own field. Mereology, as this field is called, considers questions ranging from whether a wooden table whose component parts have all had to be replaced one at a time is still that same table to whether the universe has an identity any more coherent or distinctive than a collection of bodies accelerating through space. The assumption of unity on which defenses of holistic aesthetics depend continues to be one of the most hotly contested notions in philosophy. Peter Simons, widely acknowledged as a leading authority on mereology, begins his monograph *Parts: A Study in Ontology*, by announcing that it will devote most of its four hundred pages to a critique of "Classical extensional mereology [CEM]" on the grounds that

> it asserts the existence of certain individuals, mereological *sums*, for whom existence in general we have no evidence outside the theory itself. . . . [And] the theory is not applicable to most of the objects around us, and is accordingly of little use as a formal reconstruction of the concepts of part and whole which we actually employ.[34]

Even architecture, the design of purpose-built structures, has not been immune from these debates, as Gilles Retsin demonstrates when he contends, "The parts of a building are no longer in thrall to the whole. Computational technology has evolved sufficiently to establish a new discrete architecture."[35] Scientists' attention to gunk, a mishmash with no obvious identity of its own, and fractals, patterns that are repeated on an infinite number of scales, has dramatized the fact that there is still no consensual answer to questions like "What makes a table a table and not just an assemblage of parts?" and "What is the relation between a given writer's memories and that writer's autobiography?" and "What is the difference between a collection of factually accurate statements about the past and a coherent narrative history?" and "Is identity an inherent property of objects or a presumptive projection by individual audiences?"

Mereological debates have long animated film studies and narrative theory even among scholars who, like Hitchcock, are unaware of their larger philosophical contexts. Fifteen years before Gunning's work gave the cinema of attractions widespread currency, Brian Henderson contended that the question of whether films should be consumed and judged as wholes or collections of parts was the foundational debate in film theory. In his 1971 reading of Sergei Eisenstein and André Bazin's theories as limited to "part-whole theories and theories of relation to the real," Henderson argues that "the film theory of each is in fact a theory *of the sequence*," not the whole film, which neither of them theorizes.[36]

Implicit in Henderson's categorizations is the suggestion (though he does not use these terms) that Eisenstein's theory is structural, focusing on the ways effective scenes depend on the dialectical relations among successive shots, and Bazin's phenomenological, focusing on the success of individual shots in representing physical, psychological, and spiritual reality. Many scholars of literature and film have followed Eisenstein or Bazin in rooting their theories in propositions about how unified wholes are assembled from meaningful parts or propositions about how audiences perceive the relations between parts and wholes. The commonplace that the whole is greater than the sum of its parts, a truism often inaccurately attributed to Aristotle that presumably informs Greene's reaction to *Secret Agent*, assumes that the parts are there for the sake of the whole, not vice versa.

But this is far from a universally accepted nostrum. Most of the essays in Raymond Bellour's *The Analysis of Film* drill down into a single sequence or "fragment" from given prooftexts like *The Birds* or *The Big Sleep* (1946) or *North by Northwest* in search of generalizations that have less to reveal about that particular film than about the nature of cinematic signification as such. These essays, like Bellour's essay on *Gigi* (1958), which addresses most directly the necessary but problematic relation between analyzing a film and the apparently more preliminary and innocent activity of dividing it into discrete segments, are haunted by the question, "How was I to understand [the status or operation of each individual fragment] in relation to the notions of *oeuvre* and *auteur*, of enunciation and subject, or, more broadly, of the classical model, of American cinema"?[37]

Nor are mereological questions and methodologies like those of Henderson and Bellour limited to cinema studies. The leading schools in twentieth-century literary criticism are largely defined by the ways they wrestle with the relation between parts and wholes. The leading doctrine of New Criticism, long identified with the process of close readings that searched for telling individual details, is economically summarized by Cleanth Brooks:

> The poet does not select an abstract theme and then embellish it with concrete details. On the contrary, he must establish the details, must abide by the details, and through his realization of the details attain to whatever general meaning he can attain. The meaning must issue from the particulars; it must not seem to be arbitrarily forced upon in the particulars. Thus, our conventional habits of language have to be reversed when we come to deal with poetry. For here it is the tail that wags the dog.[38]

By upending the assumption that poems are constructed top-down, Brooks implicitly raises questions about whether poems are interpreted that way, as unified structures whose larger themes govern readers' attention to individual lines and images, or as larger structures that are perceived only as they emerge through a combination of details.

Other critical schools have defined themselves largely by the different attitudes they have adopted to parts and wholes. Pioneering structuralist texts like Vladimir Propp's 1928 *Morphology of the Folktale* establish a more explicit dialectic of individual functions and events (e.g., "one of the members of a family absents himself from home") and the larger fairy tales that incorporate them by proposing that both the parts and the structures that link them are formulaic and interdependent for their meaning.[39] Ironically, the celebrated analysis of *North by Northwest* by Peter Wollen, who "was surprised how easily Propp's function and method of analysis in general could be applied to *North by Northwest*," provoked an equally detailed dissent from David Bordwell, who asserted that Wollen's "use of the concept of function creates distortions, omissions, and unconstrained analogies" that misread both Propp and Hitchcock "because most films are not wondertales."[40]

Propp's structural theory of part-whole relations is complemented by phenomenological theories that emphasize the processes by which audiences apprehend larger aesthetic unities. The most influential of these is the normative phenomenology theorized by Roman Jakobson and Roman Ingarden. But there have been several alternatives. The early Russian Formalists' work, for example, focuses more insistently on individual defamiliarizing devices that famously "make the stone *stony*" than on more general motivations that rationalize or normalize these devices through "non-artistic considerations, such as verisimilitude, psychological plausibility, and the like."[41]

Poststructuralism has largely been driven by its search for individual passages whose implications can be used to deconstruct the apparently stable structures of the works that give them meaning. Roland Barthes's deconstruction of Honoré de Balzac's story "Sarrasine" in *S/Z* raises pointed questions about both the text at hand and reading habits in general. Stephen Greenblatt's New Historicist readings of Shakespeare seek to reinsert his canonical plays as active participants in their earlier contexts by recasting their adapted stories as shelters for subversive individual parts that engage forbidden subjects. The initiatives arising from the #BlackLivesMatter and #MeToo movements typically weaponize individual details of a film or a filmmaker's life to challenge, deauthorize, or cancel individual films like *Marnie* or entire careers like that of Harvey Weinstein and Woody Allen. After years of using the climactic reveal of the murderer in *Young and Innocent* (1937) to illustrate the power of the long take to my students, I have resolved never to use this example again because it prominently displays performers in blackface, a representational scandal I had literally stopped noticing until students pointed it out to me a few years ago. Sometimes individual incidents, inside or outside a given film's boundaries, are enough to sink the whole film, or the whole career of its creator.

The Point of Studying Parts and Wholes

At the height of New Criticism's dominance over Anglo-American literary studies, W.J. Harvey, noting Charles Dickens's "impulse to exploit the full possibilities of any particular scene, situation or action without too much regard for the relevance of such local intensities to the total work of art," suggested, "We can defend in four ways the novel of episodic intensification" from criticism that "lays great stress on the organic unity of the novel and demands that no part shall be allowed autonomy if this threatens the integrity of the whole":

> First, we may admit that in some cases [like *Barnaby Rudge*] the work may fail as a whole while succeeding in some part. . . . Second, we may deny the fiat of organic unity and maintain that in *some* cases [like *Pickwick Papers*] a novel achieves no more than episodic intensification and yet possesses so much

vitality that we are content simply to accept its greatness.... Third, we may accept the idea of organic unity and yet maintain that by its standards Dickens's novels [like *Great Expectations*] are entirely successful. ... Finally, we may accept the idea of organic unity but argue that the criteria by which we judge its presence or absence have been too narrowly conceived and that there exist conventions and methods of organization which are . . . still appropriate and effective. . . . *Bleak House* is here a relevant example. Indeed, I would say that one of the reasons for its greatness is the extreme tension set up between the centrifugal vigour of its parts and the centripetal demands of the whole.[42]

The relevance of this argument to Hitchcock's films is obvious. We can easily find Hitchcock films that fit each of Harvey's categories. *Downhill* (1927), *Rich and Strange* (1931), *Waltzes from Vienna* (1933), *Jamaica Inn* (1939), and *Topaz* (1969) are examples of episodic films whose most striking sequences are more effective than the whole films that contain, or barely contain, them. There has always been livelier debate about films in Harvey's second category. British reviewer and director Lindsay Anderson, surveying Hitchcock's American films through *Rope*, found *The 39 Steps*, *The Lady Vanishes* (1938), and the 1934 version of *The Man Who Knew Too Much*— all of which subordinated the potentially "isolated delights" of their "set pieces" to "the brilliance and consistency of their narration"—superior to the Hollywood productions that followed. *Foreign Correspondent* (1940) has "excellent sequences embedded in a diffuse and vexatious story." *Saboteur* is "even more an affair of sequences." The "psychiatric background [of *Spellbound* (1945)] is futile and its Dali dream sequence merely pretentious." *Notorious* (1946) "shares with its successors, *The Paradine Case* (1947) and *Rope* (1948), the distinction of being the worst [film] of his career."[43] Years later, Leslie Halliwell implicitly dissented from his countryman's verdict by awarding a rosette to *Foreign*

Correspondent, marking it as the film "in which the person concerned was at his or her peak."[44] *Vertigo* is the clearest example of a Hitchcock film that would fit into Harvey's third category because it is characterized by organic unity in the strict sense. Many commentators would surely add *Rebecca* (1940), *Shadow of a Doubt* (1943), *Notorious*, and *Rear Window* to this category. But by far the greatest number of Hitchcock's films, especially his American productions, are organized around the programmatic tension between centrifugal and centripetal forces that Harvey finds in *Bleak House*.

Several implications can be drawn from Harvey's argument and the analogy it invites between Dickens and Hitchcock. One is that it would be a mistake to try to shoehorn all of Hitchcock's films into any single one of Harvey's four categories. Another is that, apart from members in the first category, failures that are clearly inferior to members in the other three, there are no absolute value judgments to be made among the remaining categories: some films in the second, third, and fourth categories may be better than others in that category, but there is no reason to assume that examples from any of these three categories will be *prima facie* better than examples from the other two. A third is that there is no reason to assume that these categories are exhaustive or even mutually exclusive; fans could argue at length over which category *The Lodger*, *Sabotage*, or *To Catch a Thief* (1955) belongs in. And a fourth is that no matter how we apportion Hitchcock's films among these categories—even if we decide that most of his films belong in the fourth category—none of these categories is any more Hitchcockian than the others.

All of these implications lead to the point that eluded Hitchcock detractors like Graham Greene; Hitchcock champions like Eric Rohmer, Claude Chabrol, Robin Wood, and William Rothman; philosophers like Aristotle; and Hitchcock himself, at least as he presented himself to interviewers who sought his comments on his own films. Just as there is no stable relation between individual experiences or memories and a life story, there is no ideal relation that can safely be prescribed for the relation between episodic vitality and formal unity, between parts and wholes, between fictional stories and the individual moments that make so many of these stories worth telling again and again. Hitchcock's greatest success is not his adoption of any single normative relation between set pieces and larger narrative arcs, but rather his mastery of a wide variety of approaches he took toward the dizzying profusion of possible relations.

Although there are many successful moments in even Hitchcock's least successful films, the Hitchcock films that have enjoyed the greatest commercial success have been those that fit Harvey's fourth category: those that not only exploit but ultimately resolve the tension between centrifugal and centripetal force. Hitchcock's most widely beloved films integrate the big picture with all those little pictures in order to engage both hard-core Aristotelians and audiences who have come for the attractions, the incidental, passing pleasures that will haunt their dreams even if they forget the story. These films manage to fulfill two blankly contradictory goals: to immerse the audience in their stories, as classical narrative typically seeks to do, and to use their individual attractions to play games with them, cultivating their very conscious awareness of these games—even though many of his greatest fans, once the films have ended, might well swear with perfect sincerity that they only came for the story.

The Point of Hitchcock's Greatest Films

What are Hitchcock's greatest films? Most lists of them include *The 39 Steps, The Lady Vanishes, Shadow of a Doubt, Notorious, Strangers on a Train,* and *Rear Window*—all of which, *pace* Graham Greene and Lindsay Anderson, are notable for integrating memorable moments into a larger story. Instead of focusing on any of these films, however, let me conclude by turning briefly to the three films widely considered the greatest triumphs of Hitchcock's career: *Vertigo, North by Northwest,* and *Psycho.*

Out of the films in Hitchcock's Triple Crown, the integrative approach in which dozens of individual attractions advance the story they are competing with for attention is most clearly seen in *North by Northwest*, which far more deliberately and successfully than either *The 39 Steps* or *Saboteur* presents itself as a synthesis of incidental and larger narrative attractions. If we can believe screenwriter Ernest Lehmann, his dream of writing "the Hitchcock picture to end all Hitchcock pictures" took its first step toward realization when Hitchcock told him, "I always wanted to do a chase across the faces of Mount Rushmore." Hitchcock helped Lehman take another step forward when he added weeks later, "I always wanted to do a scene . . . where the hero is standing all alone in a wide open space and there's nobody and nothing else in sight for three hundred and sixty degrees around, as far as the eye can see . . . and then along comes a tornado. No place to run."[45]

The film's plot, which developed gradually over weeks of brainstorming meetings, was expressly designed to showcase individual moments that fans of the film can recite from memory. Roger O. Thornhill (Cary Grant), forced to down enough bourbon to render him very drunk, miraculously escapes from the kidnappers who have mistaken him for the nonexistent secret agent George Kaplan. Trapped in a Plaza Hotel elevator with his mother (Jessie Royce Landis) and the kidnappers, he must endure his shame when his nod to her provokes her to ask them "You're not really trying to kill my son, are you?" and their responsive laughter spreads to everyone on the elevator but Thornhill. Rushing to the United Nations to confront Lester Townsend (Philip Ober), to whose Long Island house his kidnappers had taken him, Thornhill is on hand to see Townsend killed by a knife thrown by one of the kidnappers and then, in a moment as iconic as it is wildly improbable, is photographed standing over Townsend's body holding the murder weapon. Stowing away aboard a train bound for Chicago, Thornhill meets Eve Kendall (Eva Marie Saint), whose every encounter with him is marked as both a flirtatious set piece and another stage in the complicated romantic relationship that unfolds between them.

These moments are followed by dozens more, from the signature attack on Thornhill in an isolated cornfield by a crop dusting airplane, replacing the tornado Hitchcock had dreamed of, to the film's extended climax on Mount Rushmore, that stand out both as memorable individual moments and as episodes in the belated coming of age of the story's hero. Finally, the story is leavened throughout with winking meta-references to the star persona of Cary Grant, who can evidently prevent himself from being recognized by donning sunglasses, dressing up as a redcap porter, or shaving in a public bathroom, and who turns the startled cry of the bedridden young woman whose hospital room he has entered through the window into a melting plea for him to "stop."

Vertigo, by contrast, is a quintessential example of what happens when Hitchcock emphasizes a sustained, dreamlike narrative arc over his film's signature attractions: he produces what Hitchcock fans overwhelmingly consider his greatest film that still managed to fail with both contemporaneous reviewers and the box office, a film some fans consider absolutely perfect, while leaving many latter-day audiences cold because it never consistently delivers the attractions they secretly crave. The film does not lack for iconic moments even apart from the three fatal falls that mark the beginning, the middle, and the end of the film. Its second scene begins quietly with an expository conversation in which Scottie Ferguson (James Stewart) explains to his friend Midge Wood (Barbara Bel Geddes) why he left the police force after the opening rooftop chase in which a fellow officer died in his attempt to rescue Scottie from the rain gutter from which he was dangling. The scene builds to an unexpectedly dramatic climax as Scottie attempts to master his acrophobia by stepping onto a stool that will re-create the earlier scene on a smaller scale but ends up fainting when he looks out the window at the hilly San Francisco street below. His futile attempt to prevent Madeleine Elster (Kim Novak) from throwing herself from the top of the Mission San Juan Bautista is thwarted by his two glances down the staircase they are both running up, both rendered subjectively by a shot that simultaneously zooms in and tracks back, creating the impression of a dizzyingly extended space that became widely imitated by Brian De Palma and other filmmakers. His nightmare after Madeleine's death cuts from a series of color-filtered live-action shots to an animated sequence that dramatizes his sense of a disintegrating world. His determination to force Judy Barton (Kim Novak) to re-create the dead Madeleine is marked by a 360-degree tracking shot in which the camera circles the embracing lovers as the background behind them dissolves from Judy's apartment to Scottie's memories of his last moments with Madeleine at San Juan Bautista.

Most audiences, however, experience these moments not as discrete set pieces but as stages in Scottie's gradual immersion in the mystique of Madeleine Elster, an immersion most strikingly marked by the long, wordless sequence in which he follows her slowly by car through the streets of San Francisco as she drives to a flower shop, to the grave of Carlotta Valdes, and to the museum of the Legion of Honor, where she sits and gazes fixedly at Carlotta's portrait as Scottie stands and gazes at her. So tightly are these moments bound together that the film sharply divides audiences. Some have experienced it as a series of increasingly harrowing and ultimately shattering subjective nightmares of *déjà vu*, while others, like the attendees at Baylor University's 1996 International Hitchcock Conference, have reacted with bewilderment and disbelief when five of the six presenters in the conference's closing section agreed in pronouncing *Vertigo* Hitchcock's finest film.

The most surprising of these syntheses of incidental pleasures and sustained narrative is *Psycho*, which is rarely discussed in these terms, even though Hitchcock himself famously compared it to a funhouse whose larger structure is less important to its patrons than its incidental thrills. That is because Robin Wood's highly influential reading of the film rescued it from its earlier reputation as a series of clever but gratuitous jump scares precisely by emphasizing the thematic import of its throughline. In Wood's reading, Hitchcock uses

Marion Crane's self-conscious paranoia to introduce Norman Bates's psychosis in order to raise deeply disturbing questions about "the continuity between normal and abnormal: between the compulsive behavior of Marion and the psychotic behavior of Norman Bates." Wood concludes that "for the maker of *Psycho* to regard it as a 'fun' picture can be taken as his means of preserving his sanity; for the critic to do so—and to give it his approval on these grounds—is quite unpardonable."[46] Later commentators have routinely followed Wood in defending Hitchcock by emphasizing what Aristotle would call his plots and thoughts and sometimes his characters over the Hitchcockian equivalents of what Aristotle called Diction, Song, and Spectacle. But those apparently incidental attractions, which Hitchcock draws attention to in one interview after another, are still there, and they are still vitally important.

The exceptionally show-offy murders of Marion and Arbogast the detective are only the most obvious examples of these charged moments. Alert audiences tremble in apprehension at the moment when Marion sees her boss passing her car at a crosswalk, she notices that he's seen her as well, and the film's baleful theme music returns for the first time since the opening credits. In a subtler example that's more likely to elude first-time audiences, the cutting of the increasingly fraught parlor conversation between Marion and Norman starts off looking perfectly normal before its apparently unmotivated and disorienting low-angle framings of Norman gradually begin to make it look very strange indeed. Once Marion has died, audiences are free to take perverse pleasure in the extended moment when Marion's car, which Norman is sinking with her body inside in the swamp behind Bates Motel, suddenly comes to a halt before it finally disappears completely beneath the surface. When Lila, searching the Bates home, is suddenly terrified by the movement of what turns out to be her own mirror image, the moment invites broader consideration of the film's exploration of its characters' deepest fear, the fear of being seen as they really are.

A final memorable moment is its last line of dialogue, taken directly from Robert Bloch's novel, when Norman—or is it Mother?—prides themselves on their self-restraint in declining to swat a fly that has landed on their hand, congratulating themselves in voiceover that any possible observers would think, "She wouldn't even harm a fly." In addition, the film's dialogue is loaded with in-jokes from "Hotels of this sort aren't interested in you when you check in—but when your time is up" to "There are plenty of motels around here. You should've—I mean, just to be safe . . ." to "Mother isn't quite herself today." All of these attractions stand out as classic individual moves even as they all fit into the larger pattern of the film's game.

Audiences can oscillate, with various degrees of self-awareness, between concentrating on discrete moments like the shower scene in *Psycho* and integrating them into the larger story. They can move more or less purposefully from what Paul Ricoeur, who assumes that a "story is *made out of* events to the extent that plot *makes* events *into* a story," calls an "episodic" understanding of one discrete detail at a time to a "configurational" grasp of the entire story.[47] They can mine a film for illuminating affinities with other Hitchcock films or suggestions about the process of watching films or interpreting stories generally. And of course they can ignore the story entirely and focus entirely on their favorite Hitchcock moments, especially if they are watching a beloved film for the tenth time. But there is no predicting how any audience will react, or ought to react, during any given viewing, as Truffaut attested when he told Hitchcock about his repeated viewings of *The Lady Vanishes*: "Since I know it by heart, I tell myself each time that I'm going to ignore the plot, to examine the train and see if it's really moving, or to look at the transparencies, or to study the camera movements inside the compartments. But each time I become so absorbed by the characters and the story that I've yet to figure out the mechanics of that film."[48]

At the same time, successors to Graham Greene, assuming that the larger narrative arc of a given movie is more engaging and more important than its individual scenes or moments, continue to downplay their own persistent attraction to these smaller parts, which they routinely subordinate to their investment in larger narrative arcs. Both Hitchcock's detractors and Hitchcock's defenders, in presaging the advice of Syd Field, systematically disavow their own attraction to Hitchcock's most telling scenes and moments to the stories his movies tell.

Hitchcock's consistent attachment to the attractions that distinguish his films from so many other thrillers and his growing mastery in integrating these moments into larger stories whose power he so often disclaimed deserve closer attention from scholars and critics. It is ironic that the audiences most likely to resist this argument are the professors who inevitably treat Hitchcock films as anthologies of set pieces every time they teach them or give conference presentations or write essays about them, necessarily emphasizing some moments over others, beginning, but not ending, with the PowerPoint slides that willy-nilly reduce or equate each film with a succession of memorable moments.

One Last Point

A final test of Greene's criticism of Hitchcock is the Hitchcock films most immune to it: the twenty television segments he directed, most of them for *Alfred Hitchcock Presents* (1955–62) and *The Alfred Hitchcock Hour* (1962–65), since with a few notable exceptions their drastically abbreviated running time did not allow them to accommodate the self-contained attractions that might have disrupted the story or competed with it for attention. These episodes are so tightly unified that it would make perfect sense if latter-day Greenes who prize unity above incidental pleasures ranked them among Hitchcock's greatest achievements. Sixty years after the last episode of *The Alfred Hitchcock Hour* first aired, however, Hitchcock's work for television remains the most critically neglected aspect of his career.

Although these episodes can rarely find room for the small-scale attractions so beloved and characteristic of Hitchcock, several of them feature leading premises so striking and dominant in driving their episodes that they become attractions of their own. In "Breakdown" (originally aired on November 13, 1955), an authoritarian businessman paralyzed in a car accident struggles to persuade the people around him that he is still alive before they embalm and bury him. In "One More Mile to Go" (April 7, 1957), a man who is carrying the corpse of the wife he has just killed in the trunk of his car when he is repeatedly accosted by a police officer determined to help him get his tail light fixed. In "Lamb to the Slaughter" (April 13, 1958), a wife reacts to her police officer husband's announcement that he is leaving her for another woman by beating him to death with a frozen leg of lamb and then cooking and serving the murder weapon to the colleagues called to the scene who wonder where the weapon has gone. In "Poison" (October 5, 1958), a colonial settler who has found a deadly snake sleeping on his stomach as he lies in bed must remain perfectly still while his frenemy does all too little to help him. And in "Four O'Clock" (September 30, 1957), the inaugural episode of the short-lived television series *Suspicion*, and the only one directed by Hitchcock, a watchmaker who has rigged a bomb to explode and kill his wife at 4:00 is tied up by burglars in the basement where the bomb is ticking down the seconds. Each of these premises is so striking that it can fairly be called an attraction, a clear expression of the preference Hitchcock expressed to Truffaut for strong situations and sketchy characters over the reverse. So any hard-core fans of Greene or Aristotle—any filmgoers who still think that Hitchcock's stories trump Hitchcock's attractions—owe it to Hitchcock and themselves to pay much closer attention to these television episodes.

Toward the end of his essay, Brian Henderson asserts that "the next period of rhetorical effort [in film theory] should concentrate on formulation of better, more complex models and theories of part-whole relationships."[49] In the fifty years since Henderson made this recommendation, very few film theorists, most of them eager to move in different directions, have accepted or even acknowledged his invitation. The continuing, and largely unexamined, assumption that small-scale attractions are less important than large-scale narratives has framed the dedication to these attractions as widely reviled by critics as it is eagerly embraced by audiences. It would be a welcome development for Hitchcock studies, and for film studies generally, if Hitchcock scholars pondering the relations between his parts and his wholes could take up Henderson's invitation at last.

Notes

As always, I am deeply indebted to Sid Gottlieb for his wise and generative comments on earlier drafts of this essay.

1. Graham Greene, *Graham Greene on Film* (New York: Simon & Schuster, 1972), 75.

2. Greene, *Graham Greene on Film*, 1–2.

3. Greene, *Ways of Escape* (London: The Bodley Head, 1980), 88, 69.

4. Penelope Houston, "The Figure in the Carpet," *Sight and Sound* 32, no. 4 (Autumn 1963), quoted by Robin Wood, *Hitchcock's Films Revisited* (New York: Columbia University Press, 1989), 60.

5. Thomas Leitch, *Find the Director and Other Hitchcock Games* (Athens: University of Georgia Press, 1991), 10.

6. François Truffaut, with Helen G. Scott, *Hitchcock*, revised ed. (New York: Simon and Schuster, 1985), 121.

7. Greene, *Graham Greene on Film*, 122.

8. Syd Field, *Screenplay: The Foundations of Screenwriting*, revised and expanded ed. (New York: Dell, 1984), 132; emphasis in original.

9. James Chapman, *Hitchcock and the Spy Film* (London: I.B. Tauris, 2018), 216.

10. Tom Gunning, "The Cinema of Attraction[s]: Early Film, Its Spectator and the Avant-Garde," in *The Cinema of Attractions Reloaded*, ed. Wanda Strauven (Amsterdam University Press, 2006), 384.

11. Georges Méliès, "Importance du scénario," in Georges Sadoul, *Georges Méliès* (Paris: Seghers, 1981), 116, quoted and translated in Gunning, "The Cinema of Attraction[s]," 382.

12. Gunning, "The Cinema of Attraction[s]," 382.

13. Gunning, "The Cinema of Attraction[s]," 387.

14. Raymond Chandler, "Introduction to *The Simple Art of Murder*," in *Later Novels and Other Writings* (New York: Library of America, 1995), 1017.

15. Eric Rohmer and Claude Chabrol, *Hitchcock: The First Forty-Four Films*, trans. Stanley Hochman (New York: Frederick Ungar, 1979), ix.

16. Rohmer and Chabrol, *Hitchcock: The First Forty-Four Films*, 73, 112, 152.

17. Wood, *Hitchcock's Films Revisited*, 55, 61, 56, 133, 131, 154, 77.

18. William Rothman, *Hitchcock: The Murderous Gaze*, second ed. (Albany: State University of New York Press, 2012), xi.

19. Rothman, *Hitchcock—The Murderous Gaze*, 34.

20. Fredric Jameson, "Reading Hitchcock," *October* 23 (Winter 1982): 15.

21. Rothman, *Hitchcock—The Murderous Gaze*, 347.

22. Matthew Bilodeau, "Alfred Hitchcock Couldn't Have Cared Less About His Movies Making Sense," *Slashfilm*, April 28, 2022; online at https://www.slashfilm.com/846346/alfred-hitchcock-couldnt-have-cared-less-about-his-movies-making-sense/.

23. Thomas Leitch, "The Hitchcock Moment," *Hitchcock Annual* 6 (1997–98): 19.

24. Field, *Screenplay*, 132; emphasis in original.

25. John Buchan, *The Thirty-Nine Steps* (Boston: Houghton Mifflin, 1919), 7.

26. Truffaut, *Hitchcock,* 150–51.

27. Truffaut, *Hitchcock*, 74.

28. Truffaut, *Hitchcock*, 73; emphasis in original.

29. Truffaut, *Hitchcock*, 45, 143, 175, 195.

30. Gunning, "The Cinema of Attraction[s]," 384.

31. Truffaut, *Hitchcock*, 336.

32. S.H. Butcher, *Aristotle's Theory of Poetry and Fine Art* (New York: Dover, 1951), 23, 25, 27.

33. Butcher, *Aristotle's Theory of Poetry and Fine Art*, 33.

34. Peter Simons, *Parts: A Study in Ontology* (Oxford: Clarendon Press, 1987), 1.

35. Gilles Retsin, "In Part Whole: The Aesthetics of the Discrete," *Architectural Design*, 89, no. 5 (September/October 2019): 120-27; online at https://onlinelibrary.wiley.com/doi/10.1002/ad.2488.

36. Brian Henderson, "Two Types of Film Theory" (1971), in *A Critique of Film Theory* (New York: Dutton, 1980), 17, 23; emphasis in original.

36 THOMAS LEITCH

37. Raymond Bellour, *The Analysis of Film*, ed. Constance Penley (Bloomington: Indiana University Press, 2000), 10.

38. Cleanth Brooks, "Irony as a Principle of Structure" (1949), reprinted in *Critical Theory Since Plato*, ed. Hazard Adams, revised ed. (New York: Harcourt Brace Jovanovich, 1992), 968.

39. Vladimir Propp, *Morphology of the Folktale*, trans. Laurence Scott, ed. Louis A. Wagner, second ed. (Austin: University of Texas Press, 1968), 26.

40. Peter Wollen, "*North by Northwest*: A Morphological Analysis" (1976), reprinted in Wollen, *Readings and Writings: Semiotic Counter-Strategies* (London: Verso/New Left Books, 1982), 31; David Bordwell, "ApProppriations and ImProprieties: Problems in the Morphology of Film Narrative," *Cinema Journal* 27, no. 3 (Spring 1988): 13, 15.

41. Victor Shklovsky, "Art as Technique" (1917), reprinted in *Russian Formalist Criticism: Four Essays*, ed. Lee T. Lemon and Marion J. Reis (Lincoln: University of Nebraska Press, 1965), 12; Victor Erlich, *Russian Formalism: History–Doctrine*, 3d ed. (New Haven: Yale University Press, 1981), 194.

42. W.J. Harvey, "Chance and Design in *Bleak House*," in *Dickens and the Twentieth Century*, ed. John Gross and Gabriel Pearson (London: Routledge and Kegan Paul, 1962), 145–46.

43. Lindsay Anderson, "Alfred Hitchcock" (1949), reprinted in *Focus on Hitchcock*, ed. Albert J. LaValley (Englewood Cliffs: Prentice-Hall, 1972), 53, 55, 57.

44. Leslie Halliwell, *Halliwell's Who's Who in the Movies*, 13th ed. (New York: Harper Perennial, 1965), x. The rosette "for his understanding of the craft of the cinema, and for his virtuosity in expressing it: *Foreign Correspondent*," appears in the entry for "Hitchcock, Sir Alfred," on 197.

45. Ernest Lehman, *North by Northwest* (London: Faber and Faber, 1999), vii, viii.

46. Wood, *Hitchcock's Films Revisited*, 145, 151.

47. Paul Ricoeur, "Narrative Time," *Critical Inquiry* 7, no. 1 (Autumn 1980): 178; emphasis in original.

48. Truffaut, *Hitchcock*, 116–18.

49. Henderson, "Two Types of Film Theory," 29–30.

AMY LAWRENCE

Hitchcock's Mephisto:
O.E. Hasse and I Confess

When objections were raised to *I Confess* (1953) four years before shooting began, Alfred Hitchcock declared that "the whole purpose of this film is to show the sanctity of the confessional."[1] Even though two people are required for the Catholic rite of confession, a priest and a penitent, most descriptions of *I Confess* begin and end with the character of Father Logan (Montgomery Clift). The 1902 Paul Bourde play *Nos deux consciences*, on which the script is based, positions the priest's reaction to his situation as its dramatic core. In the play, a woman confesses that her husband has robbed and killed someone; when the priest becomes a suspect, he cannot speak because it would violate the sanctity of the confessional. In the film, it is the killer whose crime and confession initiate and propel the narrative. At every step, he increases the pressure on Father Logan by underscoring the priest's dilemma, saying in rapid succession, "You must talk or they'll hang you," and "You can't talk, you're a priest."[2] While Logan becomes a martyr-figure, maintaining his commitment to the priesthood despite persecution, Otto Keller (O.E. Hasse) follows an increasingly frantic, negative spiritual path—committing robbery and murder, concealing the truth, planting evidence, lying under oath, and killing his wife and shooting a bystander.

In a pivotal essay, Robin Wood describes many of the villains in Hitchcock's films as "fascinating" and "insidiously attractive."[3] The choice to present these characters as psychologically and morally complex (even somewhat sympathetic despite the wide range of crimes we see them commit) is one of the key ways Hitchcock's films transcend sleek entertainments and become meditations on the human condition. Otto Keller, on the other hand, has engendered unusually negative responses. For V.F. Perkins, Keller is nothing but a "colourless lump of corruption." Comparing him to classic Hitchcock villain Bruno in *Strangers on a Train* (1951), Perkins describes Keller as having the same "appalling flirtatiousness and moral sadism but none of the glamour."[4] Tracing the root-meaning of the name "Keller," Murray Pomerance adds the terms "slimy, grasping, vulgar, plain and poisonous."[5]

Because the actor Hitchcock cast as Keller was virtually unknown in the U.S., having had supporting roles in only two English-language films before *I Confess*, audiences then and now often know him only as Keller.[6] If we look at the life and career of the actor playing Keller, however, we find layers of reference that deepen any reading of the character he portrays in *I Confess*. We can see how Hasse's early career in Germany allowed Hitchcock to revisit his formative years as a director and to reexamine themes that recur throughout his work. More importantly, through Hasse Hitchcock found a way to maintain a precarious balance between good and evil, adoration and hate, fear and faith, particularly through the interplay of Hasse and Clift. Ultimately, in *I Confess* it is the relationship between Keller and the persecuted priest that becomes the means by which Hitchcock develops a nuanced exploration of Catholicism, guilt, and faith.

Hasse's Early Career in Germany

Casting O.E. Hasse as the murderer meant giving the character a historical/nationalist dimension he had never had before. In the original play, all the characters are French. The killer is named Bressaud. In a treatment written by Alma and Alfred Hitchcock in March 1948, the character is still French but has been rechristened "Andre Mallott." A year later the setting has been Anglicized, as has the character, now known as "Mel Buckle." It isn't until July of 1952 that he is given the German name "Hermann," only to have that changed ten days later in the final shooting script to "Otto Keller."[7]

At the beginning of the film, the character cites his nationality as a contributing factor in his decision to confess to Father Logan: "You gave my wife and me a home, a job, even friendship. I felt you would let me be your friend. So wonderful a thing for a refugee, a German, a man without a home." If it is important for the character to be an outsider in Canada, a displaced person, what is gained by making him a specifically German refugee? It could be a simple matter of casting. Many people note the use of Alma Reville's first name for Mrs. Keller, but "Otto" also shares a first name with the actor who plays him, Otto Eduard Hasse, billed by his initials as O.E. Hasse.[8] The change to "Otto Keller" seems to follow shortly after the hiring of Hasse, as seen in a handwritten cast list made around the time the script was finalized in the summer of 1952.

Hitchcock is said to have enjoyed working with Hasse, speaking German to him on the set.[9] They would have had a lot to reminisce about. Hasse began his career in Germany in the theater, training with Max Reinhardt in the 1920s. Hitchcock spent a formative period in Berlin in 1924, working at UFA and observing Murnau directing *Der letzte Mann* (*The Last Laugh*), in which Hasse had a small part.[10] In 1925 Hitchcock directed his first two films in Munich, the city where Hasse would establish himself as both actor and director with the theater company Die Münchner Kammerspiele beginning in 1930. Between 1933 and 1935, Hasse was in four films with Anny Ondra: *Tales of Fräulein Hoffman* [*Fräulein Hoffmanns Erzählungen*] (1933) *Little Dorrit* (1934), *The Noisy Bride* [*Die Vertauschte Braut*] (1934), and *Knockout—Ein junges Madchen, ein junger Mann* (1935). Ondra had starred in two Hitchcock films, *The Manxman* and *Blackmail* (both 1929).

In the thirties, Hasse alternated his work in the theater with multiple film appearances, mostly in supporting parts, across a variety of genres—comedies (*The Bashful*

Casanova [*Der Schuchterne*, 1936]), romances (*Dr. Crippen an Board*, 1942) (fig. 1), period films (*The Eternal Sound* [*Der Weige Klang*, 1943]) (fig. 2), musicals (*Philharmoniker*, 1944), and mysteries (*The Perpetrators Are Among Us* [*Der Täter ist unter uns*, 1944]) (fig. 3). The war years saw a flurry of work, with Hasse making between three to five films a year.[11] All of these, as Ralph Stern notes, established him as a "well-known figure in the cinema of the Third Reich."[12] (Note the official government seal in the lower right corner of Figure 3.)

There are intriguing parallels between Hasse's career in 1930s Germany and that of Gustaf Gundgrens (with whom Hasse had worked) and the character based on Gundgrens in Klaus Mann's novel *Mephisto* (1936). As described by Gundgrens's ex-lover Mann, the Gundgrens-character is an actor willing to sell his soul to the Third Reich in exchange for professional success and the chance to play the great roles of the German theater. Like Hasse and Gundgrens, the character studied with Max Reinhardt in the 1920s before establishing himself in the provinces (Munich and Hamburg respectively). Eager to become a star in Berlin, he reaches the top through political opportunism. Gundgrens himself was named artistic director of Berlin's Prussian State Theatre in 1934 where he became famous playing Mephistopheles, the role that defined his career. Hasse never achieved such prominence, and like Gundgrens and the actor in Mann's novel, his professional success rested on shaky ground. Like his life, it could be taken from him at any time.

As a gay man, Hasse was at constant risk of legal persecution under Paragraph 175, the notorious statute outlawing homosexuality.[13] When Hitler came to power in 1933, the targeting of gay men intensified. Heinrich Himmler, the head of both the criminal police and the Gestapo, was particularly zealous. Upon arrest, men suspected of being gay were subjected to "enhanced interrogation."[14] Upon conviction, some were sent to concentration camps for "indefinite detention," while others went to prison, the penalty being between six months and five years.

Figure 1

Figure 2

Figure 3

In the spring of 1939, Hasse was arrested. Having "confessed" (though it is unknown under what circumstances), he was convicted and served two months.[15] (Where he served his sentence is not clear.) The fact that Hasse was arrested at all could be considered unusual. Two years earlier, Himmler himself had declared a special exemption for "actors and artists," ordering that they "should only be detained for homosexual acts with his authorization, unless they were caught in the act."[16] Hasse's standing in theater and film clearly did not prevent his arrest, but it might account for his "relatively mild sentence" of just two months.

Hasse also, it seems, had friends in high places. Hitler was said to be "strongly impressed" with Hasse, having seen him on stage.[17] When Hasse was released from prison, the head of Munich's secret police took him aside and told him not to worry about future professional difficulties because he had been granted a "so-called special permit" by Joseph Goebbels himself.[18] Leaving Munich, Hasse took a position at the Deutsche Theatre in Prague.[19] In October 1940, Hasse was denounced again, this time by a fellow actor, and suspended. Again, Goebbels intervened and had the suspension lifted. The arbitrary nature of the implementation of anti-gay laws did not make them less threatening. Hasse was both spared and singled out, free but subject to re-arrest at any time, making him simultaneously a victim and a beneficiary of the Reich.

Hasse was also a small part of the German war machine. When the theaters were closed in September of 1944, he was drafted into the Luftwaffe. (He was 41 at the time.) In his memoirs, written in the 1970s, he minimizes his military role, describing an ill-fated engagement with American forces in France that led to his hospitalization with shrapnel wounds and eventual transfer to the Luftwaffe's main film office where he worked on training films until the war ended in May of 1945.[20] Trying to separate himself from his National Socialist-approved film career, Hasse returned to the stage in October of 1945. Taking part in what Wolfgang Schivelbusch calls the drive to revive German theater through "the

Figure 4

continuation of a great and untainted past," Hasse starred in an unimpeachable German classic, Goethe's *Urfaust*, playing Mephistopheles (fig. 4).[21]

Postwar Film Career

According to German writers Tobias Hochscherf and Christof Laucht, "the National Socialist past" cast a "persistent shadow over [film] production" in the postwar period, especially when it came to actors who had flourished in films of the Third Reich.[22] Hasse's past (legal, military, or political), however, does not seem to have posed a problem when it came to being cast in a spate of "Hollywood" films, most of which were shot outside the United States. The first, *The Big Lift* (released in the UK as *Two Corridors East*), was filmed on location in Berlin in 1950. This was followed by Anatole Litvak's *Decision Before Dawn* in 1951 and *I Confess* shot in September and October of 1952.[23] His last English-language film, *Betrayed* (1954) with Clark Gable, was shot in Holland and England and directed by Gottfried Reinhardt, son of Max. After 1954, Hasse spent the rest of his career in Europe. He did maintain a connection to Hollywood films, albeit in a limited way: when films were dubbed into German, Hasse provided the voice of nearly every major American male star, including Henry Fonda in *The Lady Eve* (1949), Clark Gable in *Honky Tonk* (1949), Humphrey Bogart in *The Caine Mutiny* (1954) and *Knock on any Door* (1954); and Spencer Tracy in *Father of the Bride* (1951), *Father's Little Dividend* (1952), and *Guess Who's Coming to Dinner* (1968).[24] Despite West Germany's maintaining the laws against homosexuality after the war, Hasse was also able to have a stable private life, enjoying a thirty-year relationship with a man beginning in 1948.[25]

In the immediate postwar period, Hasse was very aware that, as a German, he might be regarded with suspicion. Recalling the first day of shooting on *I Confess*, he wrote,

> The first rehearsal began, and I saw how every stagehand, all the lighting technicians, and everyone who was in the studio looked full of curiosity: "That's a German actor" [they were thinking], "What will the German show us?" It was breathless silence. I felt everyone . . . looking at me with interest[,] then Hitchcock called "Action."[26]

The only way for a German actor to be considered unambiguously "good" (i.e., not complicit with Fascism) was to have left Germany in the thirties. Dolly Haas, Alma Keller in *I Confess*, left with her husband director John Brahm in 1934. Those who stayed behind frequently ran into trouble resuming their careers after the war. Hildegarde Knef, for example, was cast as the female lead in *The Big Lift* but was "dropped . . .

Figure 5   Figure 6

from the project shortly before filming" began when her long-time affair with a Nazi film producer was revealed.[27] (Evidently the importance of this quickly faded, because Knef had a featured role in Hasse's next film, *Decision Before Dawn*.)

Hasse's first English-language film, *The Big Lift*, directly addresses the question of whether anyone who stayed in Germany during the war could be considered trustworthy. Take Frederica, the film's female lead. One of the women working to clear the rubble off the streets of bombed-out Berlin, she is introduced as a civilian who is grateful for the airlift, and who begins to date Danny, an American airman. When accused of complicity, she asserts her family's innocence, declaring that her father was persecuted for standing up to the Nazis. When that turns out to be a fabrication, she says she lied because she loves Danny and was afraid of losing him. That too turns out to be false when Danny finds that she was planning to use their marriage as a way to join her lover in St. Louis. This final plot twist was cut when the film was given a happy ending in an attempt to appeal to the German market.[28] The desire to recover that audience in the years after the war might also account for Hasse's prominence in German promotional material for *I Confess* (figs. 5 and 6).

This seems to be the only time Warner Bros. considered his German fame an exploitable asset.

A model of easy-going cosmopolitan charm, Hasse's character Steiber in *The Big Lift* is described in the script as simply "a Berlin type," implying a casual attitude regarding adherence to social norms. Politically pliable, Steiber is available to work for both sides in divided Berlin. Geographically flexible, he openly admits to Danny at their first meeting that he spies for the Russians but he lets the Americans know what he is doing when it is convenient. We are told that as a former actor he toured the U.S. before the war in *The Student Prince* (an unthreatening tip of the hat to pre-Nazi Germany via Old Heidelberg). While the film extols democracy in contrast to the Fascist past, there is no word on what Steiber did *during* the war, and the only example we see of Steiber's duplicity is when it is used for good. He exposes Frederica's treachery by reading her mail, spying on his German friends for his American friends.

Hasse himself takes pains in his memoirs to depict himself as neither a Nazi nor a committed opponent of the regime. He describes one single (admittedly mild) act of resistance. Sitting in a restaurant one day with a group of actors, he ad-libbed a comic sketch parodying Hitler's rhetorical style: "This skit became known and friends would request it, which was dangerous. . . . I was constantly afraid that one day my doorbell would ring and it wouldn't be the milkman."[29] As Otto Keller says when first questioned by Detective Larrue (Karl Malden): "I thought of the police. I am always afraid of the police. It is a German fear, this fear." Although he omits any mention of it in his memoirs, the knock at the door was something Hasse had experienced firsthand.

Any actor with a German background would serve in the role of Keller, including actors like Walter Slezak or Peter Lorre, who had worked with Hitchcock previously.[30] But Hasse brought something extra to the role. Various Hitchcock biographers have pointed to Hasse's first English-language film *The Big Lift* as a precursor to *I Confess* —but not for its postwar politics. Barney Hoskyns notes that "Hitchcock was especially sensitive to the sexual ambiguity of Clift and O.E. Hasse."[31] This is reiterated by Donald Spoto, who says that

Figure 7

Hitchcock was "fascinated" by actors like Clift and Hasse "who led openly homosexual or bisexual lives"—he "found the two men endlessly interesting."[32] But being gay and playing gay characters are two different things. Examining the performances of Hasse and Clift in *The Big Lift*, especially the ease with which they interact onscreen, we can see what Hitchcock might have found so intriguing.

In their first scene together, Clift's character Danny has just taken a shower while his uniform is being taken to the cleaners. Wearing the robe leant him by Herr Steiber, he goes to thank him. The chemistry between Clift and Hasse seems quite agreeably and uncomplicatedly sexual. Steiber's open, uncloseted, physically-expressed enthusiasm finds its match in Danny's relaxed receptiveness. Time and again, Steiber shifts closer and closer to the edge of his seat until his knees and hands appear intertwined with Danny's. Most remarkable is the way he can't stop touching Danny. Trying to find the words in English, Steiber rests his hand on the arm of Danny's chair, excitedly patting him on the knee then resting his hand there for a little prolonged, "unconscious" physical contact. Throughout, Danny does nothing to dissuade him, smiling and leaning closer himself as the scene proceeds (fig. 7).

Figure 8

One gesture—where Steiber points his finger and pokes Danny in the chest to emphasize a point—has a direct echo in *I Confess* when Keller climbs a ladder to be closer to Logan. Keller's life may depend on Logan's silence but his sense of security rests on Logan's emotional support and counsel, both of which are precluded by the same doctrine that guarantees a priest's silence. In the scene on the ladder, he implores Logan to speak to him: "It was *I* who confessed to you. It was *my* confession. I want you to speak to me about it. You must tell me what to do." Keller "reaches out his free hand to touch Logan's breast," a moment V.F. Perkins describes as an example of his being "driven to seek physical contact with the hero."[33] Perkins declares this gesture "unmistakable though obscured—one might think censored." The censorship is obvious. If Keller's hand ever reaches Logan's chest, we cannot see it because a bucket of paint in the foreground blocks our view (fig. 8). Perkins does not say what is "unmistakable" in this gesture and refuses explicitly to "advance a 'gay reading' (of the scene or of the film)" because, for him, doing so does not lead to a deeper understanding of the film's themes as he sees them. But recognizing erotic

Figure 9

obsession as one of the layers of Keller's motivations clarifies several issues, most importantly why Keller commits the murder that starts the film and why he confesses.

What Does Keller Want?

Keller attempts to explain the murder he has committed in a speech divided across three scenes: his first encounter with Logan in the church, the beginning of his confession, and its conclusion in the scene with his wife. In this speech he advances three possible motives. First: "It was the money." He tells Alma, "I lie awake, night after night, and I think all we need is two thousand dollars. With two thousand dollars we can start a new life." When the police later say that some money was left at the scene of the crime, it suggests that Keller tried to assuage his conscience by taking only the $2,000 he says he needs. In a rarely reproduced publicity still, Keller shows Alma a fistful of cash (fig. 9). This moment was evidently deleted from the film where money-as-motive soon disappears. Although

Otto says explicitly that he cannot return the money (for fear of the police), neither does he spend it.

The second proposed motive is that he wanted the money for his wife's sake. He tells Logan, "It was my wife—working so hard—It breaks my heart." As the confession continues into the next scene, with Alma taking the place of Logan, Keller tells her, "How could I watch you work so hard?" Again, although he keeps the money, he does not spend it on Alma. As for his devotion to her, by the end of the scene he has moved from dependence to dominance bordering on contempt. When she suggests the police will come and that Father Logan will talk, Keller rises up, clutching her arms, and raises his voice: "He cannot tell them. Can't you understand that!"

The third thing Keller wants is for Logan to be his friend. In the first part of their encounter, Keller recounts how Logan offered "my wife and me a home, a job, even friendship." (Alma is almost immediately excluded as he proceeds to say, "I felt you would let *me* be your friend.") Aware that he has betrayed Logan's kindness, he says, "You will hate me," revealing his simultaneous desire for Logan's good opinion and his fear of rejection. Abruptly rising, he states that he wants to confess.

Unlike Logan, whose every utterance is measured and thoroughly thought-through, Keller acts on impulse, often in ways that are contradictory or not in his best interest. Confessing, for example, has no apparent upside for Keller. Firstly, he does not seem motivated by a true religious desire for absolution. Immediately following his confession to Logan, he tells Alma that he does not intend to follow the priest's instruction to return the money and he will not turn himself in: "I can't give myself up. I can't. They would hang me." As soon as he has confessed, Keller begins to fear that Logan will betray his trust, just as Keller has betrayed Logan's. What the confession does do for Keller is secure a bond between himself and Logan. Robbing and killing someone has given Keller an excuse to go to Logan and place his life—and his soul—in Logan's hands. According to Catholic doctrine, a request for confession is a demand a priest

Figure 10

cannot refuse, meaning that Keller knows Logan can only submit, thus being manipulated into sharing Keller's secret.

As spreading of the confession over three scenes illustrates, Keller's relationship with Logan takes precedence over his relationship with Alma. After the murder, he talks to Logan first, Alma second. Later, when he approaches Logan on the ladder, Alma interrupts. Keller quickly jerks his hand back and steps away as if to disavow something forbidden. Alma's position as an intruder is underscored as she is shown literally coming between the two men, creating a triangle with herself as the least important member. The browbeaten, perpetually worried Alma is relegated to the background, between her husband and someone who has become more important to him than his wife. There is a similar shot in *The Big Lift* where the woman is also a frustrated witness to the men's interaction (fig. 10).

By the end of *I Confess*, Keller again reveals how Logan and Alma have become interchangeable. After shooting Alma and threatening to shoot Logan, he asks, "Why will I not shoot you? Because you call me 'Otto' in such a friendly way? Like Alma used to call me 'Otto'?" Raising his gun, he is shot by the police. Enacting the mandatory tragic ending of a mid-century gay love story, he dies in Logan's arms, openly embraced only in death.

Queering the Texts

After his confession, Keller "discovers" the body of the murdered man and calls the police. Returning to the rectory, he waits for a moment in the doorway, watching Father Logan humbly painting a wall (fig. 11). In this quiet, pivotal moment, we see Logan through Keller's eyes (fig. 12). It is the first time Keller has seen Logan since the confession and what he sees is not a priest in a cassock but a young man in civilian clothes, vulnerable, beautiful. (Logan's shadow, with an arm outstretched and a vertical shaft through the middle, can also be read as an image of a crucifixion.) Throughout the film Clift's character is most sexually available when he is not wearing a cassock, for example, when Ruth (Anne Baxter), kisses him on the hillside, they are caught in the rain, and she sees him in the summer house the next morning. (These are also the scenes when he is referred to as "Michael" and not "Father Logan.") No doubt this placated the Production Code administrators, but it adds an extra dimension of sexual attraction to the shot/counter-shot of Figures 11 and 12. As in the scene in *The Big Lift* when, without a word, Steiber removes his jacket while contemplating Danny in a robe, Keller moves into the space, shedding his jacket and keeping his eyes on Logan the whole time.

Identifying Keller's obsession with Logan as simply that of a gay man in love with someone unobtainable oversimplifies the range of contradictions inherent in Keller's actions. In her book on Montgomery Clift, Elisabetta Girelli argues the importance of moving past gay/straight binaries and embracing the broader, category-expanding concept of "queer." She argues that a queer perspective emphasizes how identities—sexual and otherwise—are "culturally produced, . . . constructed and acquired and constantly in the process of being constituted and reconstituted. Individual identity, therefore, is not innate or coherent, but rather assumed, multiple, and fragmented."[34] This can be a positive, creative flux or it can be a self-destructive process of disintegration, as shown in *The Big Lift* and *I Confess* respectively.

Figure 11

Figure 12

In *The Big Lift*, Hasse's character "embodies ambiguity" with his unusually fluid identity—a trait or skill set he offers to share with Danny, as exemplified by their exchange of clothes.[35] First seen wearing Steiber's robe, Danny later wants to leave the apartment. Steiber wordlessly begins to undress, offering the young American his jacket and pants (see fig. 10). In order to inhabit this new identity, Danny must violate military rules against being out of uniform. He has to dodge MPs by posing as an entertainer (like Steiber the actor), move through the Soviet zone without being apprehended (like Steiber the Russian spy), and allow himself to be passed off as the enemy (a wounded German war veteran—a term that might apply to Steiber but definitely applies to Hasse). Meanwhile, for the next few scenes, Steiber dons the robe Danny wore.

In *I Confess*, Keller is introduced wearing the clothes that Logan wears. Hurrying away from the scene of the crime, he pauses to quickly take off a priestly cassock, distancing himself from an identity fundamentally at odds with who he is.[36] We cut to Logan unbuttoning his cassock as he begins to disrobe. Looking out a window, he stops for a moment when he sees a man entering the church. Instead of retiring for the night, he decides to go down to the church, prioritizing his duty as a priest—something he will need to reaffirm repeatedly throughout the film.

Where Steiber impishly encourages Danny to take risks by experimenting with different identities, Keller tries to impose an identity on Logan that violates who Logan is—and he is not the only one. Keller's obsession with Logan is paralleled by that of Ruth, the woman Logan dated before he decided to become a priest. Each sees Logan as central to his or her future: Keller for his very life and Ruth for her happiness. Both are married to long-suffering spouses who they depend on but also take for granted. Keller ultimately kills his wife, while Ruth humiliates her husband publicly and privately. Each is frustrated by Logan's self-containment, his refusal to indulge their visions of a personal as opposed to a pastoral relationship. Most importantly, both override Logan's right to define himself by speaking for him. On the ferry, Ruth tells Logan, "You're in love with me. You've always been in love with me. You haven't changed." Hearing that Logan is about to be arrested, Keller, wearing white and dropping wilted flowers from a bouquet, looks like a jilted bride desperately following the man who has literally left him at the altar.[37] Pursuing Logan down hallway after hallway, Keller pelts him with accusations relating to his own fears:

> Perhaps you will point your finger at me. Perhaps you will say: It is Keller. That's what you'll do, is it? You are a coward after all. You are frightened. Maybe they will hang you instead of me and that frightens you.

Attempting to persuade Logan that they are the same (that they think alike and share the same ignoble feelings), Keller hammers at Logan's composure until it almost breaks, even if breaking Logan would mean Keller's destruction. Finally, Logan turns on him, not saying a word, and Keller recoils. Assuming that Logan, deep down, is as craven as he is himself, Keller immediately sets about framing him for the murder.

Compared to Keller and Ruth, Logan's use of language is precise, correct, and unrevealing. Where Keller's use of the term "friend" can be taken to imply a great deal, Logan's use of it is strictly circumscribed. Asked at the trial about his relationship with Ruth in the past, Logan describes them as having been "good friends," falling far short of Ruth's willful insistence on a grand romance. Both Keller and Ruth find Logan an ideal surface onto which to project an idealized image of themselves (i.e., someone loved by him). When threatened with the loss of that imaginary union, they each turn on him, consciously or unconsciously implicating him in the crime. While making *I Confess*, Karl Malden famously said that Montgomery Clift had the face of a saint.[38] But not everyone reacts positively to a saint. They can be remote, unreachable, literally on a pedestal. As Keller asks Logan, gazing up toward him on the ladder, "Aren't you human? Haven't you ever been afraid?" Meant to inspire, saints can do the opposite, tempting people to try to pull them down.

The freeing fluidity of "queer" identity exemplified by Steiber and Danny in *The Big Lift* becomes devastatingly unstable in Hitchcock's film. In this way, *I Confess* hovers between a classic mid-century depiction of homosexuality-as-neurosis and a subversive undermining of phallic masculinity. According to pre-Stonewall psychoanalytic theories, as Brett Farmer notes, "the gay subject" is "positioned in a network of desire *vis-à-vis* the father" (or as Keller says, "My only friend, *Father* Logan"). Unlike the heterosexual, the gay subject "plays out . . . a transgressive scenario [such as committing murder dressed as a priest] in which the father's position is undermined" (e.g., Logan being suspected, arrested, put on trial, and jeered by a mob).[39] Sitting in court, watching the proceedings, Keller has succeeded in his project to "displace and undo the father's position of phallic privilege." Logan has been repositioned as spectacle, turned into "'a passive object' of and for the gay subject's erotic desires."

Keller is torn between trying to subvert the authority of the symbolic father/priest and wanting to *be* Logan. Testifying at the trial, Keller assumes Logan's good qualities by re-casting the original confession scene with himself in the role of the compassionate friend trying to console a guilty man kneeling in the dark. But idealizing Logan destabilizes Keller's identity, bringing home to him his own inadequacy. Logan as played by Clift is, effortlessly, everything Hasse's Keller cannot be: young, beautiful, and good. Wanting to become one with his ideal, Keller also needs to destroy him if he is to have any hope of continuing to exist. But destroying the person he wants to become is just another form of self-annihilation.

"Where Is My Alma?"

Although Hitchcock described *I Confess* as celebrating a priest's dedication to his vocation, it is Keller's struggle with faith that sets the narrative in motion and provides the film's climax.[40] Hitchcock throws Logan's religious devotion into relief by featuring its opposite—a man who wants to believe but cannot. In terms of faith, Logan suffers and may waver but inevitably does the right thing. Keller, on the other hand, is wracked with contradictions. Alternately panic-stricken and domineering, he mentions his love for his wife frequently but treats her with disdain and ultimately kills her.

Sentimental and cold-blooded, weak yet murderous, Keller is desperate to feel safe. Convinced that Logan must remain silent ("You can't tell them as long as you are a priest"), he is nevertheless plagued by doubt. Keller is pulled under by his lack of faith not only in Logan but in the possibility that anyone could be Logan: trustworthy, reliable in the face of opprobrium and threats of imprisonment, and willing to die in adherence to his vows. In the last scene when Keller's doubts seem to be confirmed, he is almost triumphant. Confronting Logan, he revels in abusing him:

> My only friend, Father Logan! How kindly he hears my confession. Then, a little shame, a little violence— that's all it takes to make him talk! It was too much for you, eh? You're a coward like all other people, aren't you? A hypocrite like all the rest!

According to Chabrol and Rohmer, Keller, having made Logan "the mirror of [his] conscience," sees in that mirror "his own deformed and exposed image."[41]

Unable to maintain the distinction between their identities, Keller reflexively projects his guilt onto Logan. When Logan tells him that Alma is dead ("You killed her"), Keller replies, "It is your fault; I loved her." One of the most perverse lines in the film, Keller's response is directly contradicted by what we have just seen: Keller shooting Alma in order to save himself from being exposed. For Keller, Logan is responsible in two ways: being so sympathetic at the trial that Alma betrays her husband to clear the priest, and, more importantly, by making her superfluous when he unwittingly took Alma's place as Keller's soulmate, his "alma." Saying that he loved Alma makes it clear that loving someone does not stop Keller from killing them, which in turn makes it possible for him to kill Logan. When Logan asserts that Keller will not shoot him, Keller again puts Logan in his wife's place. "Why will I not shoot you? Because you call me 'Otto' in a such a friendly way? Like Alma used to call me 'Otto'?"

Keller's confusing Logan and Alma might put Logan's life at risk, but when Keller equates Logan with himself it is to welcome him to a desolate world of isolation and suicidal despair. Denying the obvious ("She can't be dead"), Keller tells Logan they are the same:

> Then I am as alone as you are. . . . To kill you now would be a favor to you. You have no friends. What has happened to your friends, eh father? They mob you, they call at you. It would be better you were as guilty as I am. Then they would shoot you, quickly, and you mustn't suffer much.

Raising his gun, Keller is shot by the police. He dies in Logan's arms, calling for help and forgiveness.

As we saw in *The Big Lift*, the question of forgiveness has specific historical resonance in the postwar period, something underlined by Hitchcock's casting of a "well-known figure in the cinema of the Third Reich." "Forgive me" are the last words spoken to priest and World War II veteran Michael Logan by both Keller and Alma, who asks for forgiveness in German. Attention is drawn back to the war when absolution is requested by the man who actively tried to destroy Logan and by his wife, a civilian who has been complicit by her silence. Keller's dying at the foot of a stage also reminds us of actor Hasse's background in German theatre, including his immediate postwar performance as Mephistopheles. Like Goethe's Mephistopheles, Keller puts Logan to the test: undermining him, tempting him, pushing him to his limit, making him suffer, punishing him for being young, beautiful, and good.[42] ("You're so good. It is easy for you to be good," he says.) Spiritually, however, it is Keller who is the more tragic figure. Logan is ultimately recognized as having maintained his commitment to the priesthood despite persecution. Keller, on the other hand, ends where he began—begging for forgiveness from a figure, and perhaps a God, whose goodness he could never fully believe in. As Keller, Hasse establishes the crucial ambivalence about religious faith at the heart of Hitchcock's *I Confess*.

Notes

I would like to thank Ulrike Rainer for her help in translating German sources.

1. Hitchcock to John Schuyler, telegram, November 30, 1948, Production Code Administration (PCA) files, Margaret Herrick Library, The Academy of Motion Picture Arts and Sciences.
2. All dialogue quoted in my essay is transcribed from the film.
3. Robin Wood, "The Murderous Gays: Hitchcock's Homophobia," in *Hitchcock's Films Revisited,* rev. ed. (New York: Columbia University Press, 2002), 347.
4. V.F. Perkins, "*I Confess*: Photographs of People Speaking," *CineAction* 52 (June 2000): 30.
5. Murray Pomerance, *An Eye for Hitchcock* (New Brunswick: Rutgers University Press, 2004), 287n20.
6. Hasse's previous English language films were *Decision Before Dawn* (1951) and *The Big Lift* (1950). *Decision Before Dawn* ranked 38 out of the top 50 grossing films of the year (*Strangers on a Train* was 19). The year it was released, *The Big Lift* ranked 125; see the yearly rankings available at www.ultimate rankings.com.
7. The Warner Bros. Archive at USC has an October 29, 1952, account compiled by Hitchcock assistant Barbara Keon detailing every person who contributed to the development of the project. See Amy Lawrence, *The Passion of Montgomery Clift* (Berkeley and Los Angeles: University of California Press, 2010), 302n85.
8. Hasse is listed as "Hermann," Clift as "Michael," Gusti Huber as "Mrs. Hermann," and Karl Malden and Anne Baxter as Larrue and Ruth. (Note on stationery from "The St. Regis, Fifth Avenue, Fifty-fifth Street, New York" [no date], *I Confess* file, Warner Bros. Archive, USC.)
9. "Miss Baxter, Mr. Clift . . . speak French and Mr. Hitchcock also speaks German when he talks with actor Hasse." See "Tourists in Quebec Throng to see Hitchcock Make Movie," *Boston Sunday Globe,* September 14, 1952. A French-language Canadian paper covering the shooting of *I Confess* in Quebec City reports that Baxter's French was excellent, but Clift spoke with more difficulty. It is not mentioned whether Clift spoke German, having spent five months Berlin in 1947 while shooting *The Search* and in Berlin again for *The Big Lift*, shot in 1949 and released April 1950.

10. Uncredited and unidentified, the character Hasse most resembles is the bellhop operating the revolving door in *Der letzte Mann*'s famous opening shot.

11. Hasse appeared in four films in 1941, three in 1942, three in 1943, and five in 1944.

12. Ralph Stern, "'*The Big Lift*' (1950): Image and Identity in Blockaded Berlin," *Cinema Journal* 46, no. 2 (Winter 2007): 88n17.

13. Paragraph 175 reverted to pre-1935 levels after the war. It ended in East Germany in 1989 and, after a series of reforms, was finally rescinded in West Germany in 1994.

14. Alan Steinweis, *Art, Ideology, and Economics in Nazi Germany* (Chapel Hill: University of North Carolina Press, 2017), 150; Melanie Murphy, "Homosexuality and the Law in the Third Reich," in *Nazi Law—From Nuremberg to Nuremberg* (London: Bloomsbury Academic, 2017), 116; and Michael Schwartz "Verfolgte Homosexuelle—oder Lebenssituationen von LSBTQI? (Persecution of homosexuals—or life circumstances of LGBTQI?), in *Homosexuals under National Socialism: New Research Perspectives on the Life Circumstances of Lesbian, Gay, Bisexual, Transsexual, and Intersexual Persons from 1933 to 1945*, ed. Michael Schwartz (Oldenbourg: DeGruyter, 2014), 388.

15. "Entertaining the Troops," *Archiv-Blätter 9* (Stiftung Archiv der Akademie Der Kunste, 2003), 74, online at https://www.filmportal.de/en/person/o-e-hasse_efc0caa3e8f403c 1e03053d50b372d46. Hasse was dismissed from the Münchner Kammerspielen in January 1939 and forbidden to appear in the government-controlled theaters in Germany.

16. https://en.wikipedia.org/wiki/Persecution_of_homosexuals_in_Nazi_Germany.

17. https://de.wikipedia.org/wiki/O.E.Hasse. This source mentions Shaw's *Caesar and Cleopatra*, though Hasse's credits list him as having directed the play (September 20, 1938), rather than starring in it (O.E. Hasse, *O.E.: Unvollendete Memoiren [Unfinished Memoirs]*, [Munich: C. Bertelsmann, 1979], 289). Hasse describes meeting Hitler in July 1937 with a group of other actors. "Goebbels introduced us" (57). Hitler asked him about his role in Lessing's *Minna von Barnhelm*: "I sat there stunned. Thank God I never met him again" (59).

18. https://de.wikipedia.org/wiki/O._E._Hasse. Works cited here include Hasse's memoirs; Hans Knudsen's *O.E. Hasse* (Berlin: Rembrandt-Verlag, 1960); and Jörg Schöning "O.E. Hasse—Schauspieler," in *CineGraphLexikon zum deutschsprachigen Film* (Lieferung 1, 1984).

19. As Anselm Heinrich points out, the Nazis gave particular importance to German language theatrical productions in occupied territories; Prague had come under German rule with the annexation of the Sudetenland the year before. After the occupation of Prague, for example, the government's direct financial investment resulted in a rise in theatrical employees "from 110 in 1939 to almost 500 in 1943." Although the stated purpose of these productions was to promote German classics, Heinrich argues that most "audiences were entertained with an ordinary, brutally trivial repertoire at give-away prices." Overall, he concludes, "the performances of German *Kulturgüter* cannot be separated from the context of terror in which they were staged." See "Theatre as Weapon of War: German Language Theatres Across Occupied Europe During WWII," *Critical Stages/Scènes critiques*, no. 7 (June 2023), online at https://www.critical-stages.org/27/theatre-as-weapon-of-war-german-language-theatres-across-occupied-europe-during-wwii/.

20. "Hasse was drafted by [the] Wehrmacht but was soon deployed to 'Hauptfilmstelle der Reichsluftwaffe' to participate in the short documentary film 'Rettet den deutschen Wald' (*Save the German Forest*)"; see "Entertaining the Troops," 74, and Hasse, *O.E.: Unvollendete Memoiren*, 89-91.

21. Wolfgang Schivelbusch, *In a Cold Crater: Cultural and Intellectual Life in Berlin, 1945-48*, trans. Kelly Barry (Berkeley and Los Angeles: University of California Press, 2018), 59.

22. Tobias Hochscherf and Christoph Laucht, "Censorship, Scripts, Suppression, and Selection: Twentieth Century-Fox and the Story of the Berlin Airlift in *The Big Lift* and *Es began mit einem Kuss* (*It Started with a Kiss*), 1950-1953," *Film History* 31, no. 3 (2019): 94.

23. According to Paul Rotha, *Decision Before Dawn* was shot "wholly on location in Germany, including I believe in the Munich studios" (*Sight and Sound* 21, no. 2 [October-December 1951]: 77). *I Confess* was shot in Quebec City with "post-recorded dialogue for Hasse" scheduled for November 3, 1952, in Hollywood (*I Confess* file, Warner Bros. Archive, USC).

24. All dates specify the year the film was released in West Germany. "Entertaining the Troops," 89-90. He also dubbed Gene Kelly in *The Three Musketeers* (released 1950), George Sanders in *All About Eve* (German release 1952), as well as British actors Robert Donat (*The Winslow Boy*) and Charles Laughton in *Mutiny on the Bounty* (both released in Germany in 1951). Hasse insisted that "dubbing of the voices of foreign actors is not only a technical affair."

"The actor who speaks the text must have a fine ear for the voices of the original actors. There's also a certain skill in the treatment of the word. . . . Sensitivity for the role is necessary as if one had originally played it oneself" (Hasse, *O.E.: Unvollendete Memoiren*, 33-34).

25. https://en.wikipedia.org/wiki/O._E._Hasse. After Hasse's death in 1977, his partner Max Wiener became a prominent AIDS activist.

26. Hasse, *O.E.: Unvollendete Memoiren*, 151.

27. Hochscherf and Laucht, "Censorship, Scripts, Suppression, and Selection," 94.

28. Hochscherf and Laucht, "Censorship, Scripts, Suppression, and Selection," 94.

29. Hasse, *O.E.: Unvollendete Memoiren*, 86. The skit titled "Hitler on the Radio" featured a rousing speech on the subject of "the Great German Ashtray."

30. Like Hasse, Slezak had worked in German film at the same time as Hitchcock. In *Michael* (1924), he plays a handsome young man loved by an older artist in Carl Theodor Dreyer's landmark in gay cinema. In that performance, Slezak, like Hasse, offered Hitchcock an early glimpse of homoeroticism. Peter Lorre also played characters who could be considered queer, including Joel Cairo in *The Maltese Falcon* (1941) and the seemingly asexual Mr. Moto in eight films between 1937-39.

31. Barney Hoskyns, *Montgomery Clift: Beautiful Loser* (New York: Grove Weidenfeld, 1991), 100.

32. Donald Spoto, *The Dark Side of Genius: The Life of Alfred Hitchcock* (New York: Little Brown & Co., 1983), 340. Hitchcock's hostility toward Clift on the set of *I Confess* has been widely reported. The reasons given include Clift's drinking, his alleged use of a time-consuming Method approach to acting, and his reliance on an acting coach whose presence on the set Hitchcock took as an affront to his authority. Hasse, on the other hand, praises Hitchcock, the cast and the crew, but "especially Montgomery Clift," calling him a "charming human being and a serious, brilliant actor" and "the best partner an actor could ever hope to have" (Hasse, *O.E.: Unvollendete Memoiren*, 31).

33. Perkins, "*I Confess*: Photographs of People Speaking," 39.

34. Elisabetta Girelli, *Montgomery Clift: Queer Star* (Detroit: Wayne State University Press, 2014), 20.

35. Stern, "'*The Big Lift*' (1950)," 73.

36. Hitchcock's *Murder!* (1930) also begins with the killer appearing at the scene of the crime wearing a uniform that puts him

above suspicion while making him invisible as an individual. Handel Fane (Esme Percy) dresses like a police officer, Keller like a priest. Like Keller, Fane is ostensibly motivated to commit murder out of concern for the woman he loves. The bulk of the film, however, focuses on how he is simultaneously drawn to and afraid of the elegant, sophisticated Sir John (Herbert Marshall). As with Logan and the implicit promise of absolution, attention, and friendship, the theatrical producer Sir John has the power to grant Fane's desire to be an actor on the "legitimate" stage, bestowing on him the respect of a professional peer. At the same time, the man each killer idolizes could destroy him. Eventually trapped, both Keller and Fane reveal themselves in a blaze of theatrical excess. Fane, a cross-dressing trapeze artist, intentionally falls to his death while Keller commits suicide-by-cop while standing in a ballroom in front of a stage.

37. Hitchcock was told to cut the line "I'm going to be arrested" because the Breen office worried that it might seem as if Logan was discussing matters raised in the confessional. Having just been informed by Ruth that he is about to be arrested, his restating it does not depend on anything he has learned from Keller in private. (PCA files, "*I Confess,*" Margaret Herrick Library, Academy of Motion Picture Arts and Sciences.)

38. Karl Malden, with Carla Malden, *When Do I Start?* (New York: Simon & Schuster, 1997), 229.

39. Brett Farmer, summarizing Otto Fenichel's *The Psychoanalytic Theory of Neurosis* (1945), in *Spectacular Passions: Cinema, Fantasy, Gay Male Spectatorships* (Durham: Duke University Press, 2000), 203.

40. Hitchcock to John Schuyler, telegram, November 30, 1948. PCA files, Margaret Herrick Library, The Academy of Motion Picture Arts and Sciences.

41. Claude Chabrol and Eric Rohmer, *Hitchcock,* trans. Stanley Hochman (New York: Frederick Ungar, 1979), 114.

42. Girelli, *Montgomery Clift,* 101. Girelli describes Clift at this point in time as looking "exquisite and nearly perfect" (3). When Logan first walks through the church holding a candle, she says, "For a moment his beauty is made to look surreal, bathed in light" (101).

GARRETT A. SULLIVAN, JR.

Taming Marnie: *Hitchcock's Shakespeare, Shakespeare's Hitchcock*

In a 1972 essay, George Kaplan decries Robin Wood's tendency in his pathbreaking *Hitchcock's Films* (1965) to compare the Master with the Bard:

> What exactly *does* [Wood] wish [those comparisons] to convey? He is careful not to be tied down to any definite commitment to the opinion that Hitchcock is as great an artist as Shakespeare. Yet one feels that, if Wood were compelled to recognize just *how* inferior to Shakespeare Hitchcock is, he would be forced to modify his whole account and evaluation of the films fairly drastically.[1]

At the core of Hitchcock's relative inferiority, Kaplan suggests, is his disinterest in producing "any presentation of normality, or in the definition of norms" (51); "Hitchcock's art . . . is most intense when it leaves daily reality, the 'normal,' behind to explore unnatural relationships and extreme mental states, especially the obsessive-compulsive, in a kind of abstraction only cursorily disguised as naturalism" (48). Among several other films, *Marnie* (1964) offers Kaplan a case in point: "Normal life, for Hitchcock the artist, is always pretty empty. One fears that, once Marnie is cured, Mark (and Hitchcock) may cease to find her at all interesting. Her animal-like, *vital* qualities seem to be presented as the product of neurosis" (52; emphasis in original). It is also to *Marnie* that Kaplan turns in the essay's final paragraph, to explain why Wood's Shakespeare-Hitchcock comparison is misguided:

For Hitchcock is, at his best, a great artist, if of neither the kind nor degree that Wood implies. His work is too far removed from any healthy concept of normality, or from any sense of *potential* norms, to have the kind of Shakespearean centrality Wood suggests. *Marnie* is not, even remotely, *The Winter's Tale.* (53; emphasis in original)

What makes this critique of both Wood and Hitchcock particularly interesting is that "George Kaplan" is a pseudonym for Wood himself (the name, of course, is that of Roger Thornhill's non-existent alter ego in *North by Northwest* [1959]). Indeed, this essay is a spoof, albeit one that correctly notes Wood's repeated yoking of Hitchcock and Shakespeare in *Hitchcock's Films,* published subsequently in revised and expanded editions as *Hitchcock's Films Revisited.*[2] More broadly, Kaplan's piece operates in two almost contradictory ways: on the one hand, it is the vehicle by which Wood pokes fun at wrongheaded interpretations of the original *Hitchcock's Films*; and, on the other, it serves to acknowledge what he has come to see as that book's failings. As for the way *Hitchcock's Films* takes up Shakespeare, Wood does not concern himself, as Kaplan does, with the relative greatness of the two artists; the most sustained comparison centers instead on the cinema and theater as commercial enterprises, and movies and plays as popular art forms.[3] Similarly, while Kaplan suggests that *Marnie* falls far short of *The Winter's Tale,* Wood links the two on the basis not of their merits but of their shared status as adaptations.[4] And if Wood references *Macbeth* as part of his analysis of *Psycho* (1960), it is to illuminate an aspect of the film, not to evaluate the comparative achievements of the two artists who produced these works. And yet, while Kaplan misrepresents the uses to which Shakespeare is put in Wood's book, he also articulates, by way of Shakespeare's difference from Hitchcock, an element of Wood's worldview that, by 1972, he had repudiated. In the preface to the revised edition of *Hitchcock's Films Revisited*, Wood contends that his 1965 book was animated by "the commitment to what I had been taught to see as 'normality,' inseparably fused with my knowledge that [as a closeted gay man] I would never be 'normal.'"[5] "George Kaplan," spokesperson for a "healthy concept of normality," voices an ideology that, by 1972, Wood had come to reject. Most important for our purposes is the fact that Kaplan associates Shakespeare with that ideology while suggesting Hitchcock deviates from it, and is a lesser artist for doing so.

It seems safe to assume that Kaplan's Shakespeare—the poet of healthy normality—is not Wood's; as he surely recognized, a number of Shakespeare's works, like Hitchcock's, "explore unnatural relationships and extreme mental states." And yet, to many, Kaplan's view of the Bard would appear unexceptional. That is part of Wood's (very inside) joke. He implies that Shakespeare has been so thoroughly assimilated by mid-twentieth-century Western culture that those aspects of his work that share an affinity with Hitchcock's are less obvious than they should be. Or, to put it differently, he suggests that the "unhealthy" elements of Shakespeare—the violence or perversity of his work, the challenge it poses to the patriarchal status quo—have been occluded in favor of his putative universality and normality. While Kaplan differentiates Hitchcock from Shakespeare, Wood intimates an affinity between the two. Significantly, that affinity is located on terrain that, according to Kaplan, is more usually construed as Hitchcockian than Shakespearean.[6]

As we have seen, both Wood and Kaplan relate *Marnie* to *The Winter's Tale*. However, according to Charlotte Chandler, Hitchcock himself compared his film to a different Shakespeare play: "'*Marnie* was *The Taming of the Shrew*,' Hitchcock told me, 'but the public didn't notice.'"[7] Insofar as the two works concern themselves with transgressive women whose husbands explicitly set out to "tame" them, the comparison makes intuitive sense, and it has occasionally been noted by Hitchcock scholars.[8] And yet, for Hitchcock to say that *Marnie* "was" *The Taming of the Shrew* is for him to speak imprecisely; Shakespeare's play is not a source for the film, or even for the novel it was based upon, Winston Graham's *Marnie* (1961).[9] How, then, are we to think about the relationship between the sixteenth-century play and the twentieth-century movie? What did Hitchcock see in Shakespeare's play when he drew an equivalence between the two works?

My essay will take Hitchcock's statement as an invitation to consider *Marnie* and *The Taming of the Shrew* in relation to one another. My objective will be less to itemize similarities between the two works, though there will be some of that, than to consider how each might be read through the lens of the other—as Hitchcock himself did in talking to Chandler. In doing so, I will also necessarily not attend to many of the striking dissimilarities between the two works when it comes to characterization, tone, genre, medium, and so on. To approach Shakespeare's play with *Marnie* in mind is to consider how Petruccio's efforts at taming, while putatively marked by his sexual self-abnegation, have a sadistic dimension that chimes with Mark's sexual fetishism; while to examine *Marnie* in light of *The Taming of the Shrew* is to sharpen our sense of how the movie explores the tensions between marriage as an interpersonal bond and as a property relation. Both works put pressure on patriarchal authority, but they do so in ways that are conditioned by their particular historical moments: *Marnie*'s treatment of marital rape harmonizes with and differs from *The Taming of the Shrew*'s interrogation of the nature and limits of coverture. In broader terms, placing *Marnie* and *The Taming of the Shrew* in dialogue with one another allows us to think more deeply about the matter raised by George Kaplan (and Robin Wood before—and as—him): the relationship between Shakespeare, Hitchcock and "normality" under patriarchy.

* * * * * *

Shortly after having robbed the safe at Rutland Publishing, Marnie Edgar (Tippi Hedren) is confronted by Mark Rutland (Sean Connery), who, having tracked her from Philadelphia, forces her to return there with him. On the drive, Mark poses questions about Marnie's past that she responds to with a combination of truths, half-truths, and lies. It is during this interrogation that he informs her that the two are going to be wed. If later in the same conversation he tells Marnie he is proposing to her, which would imply she has some say in the matter, the way he first broaches the topic makes clear that she has no choice:

> When we get home, I'll explain that we had a lover's quarrel, that you ran away, that I went after you and brought you back. That'll please Dad, he admires action. Then I'll explain that we're going to be married before the week is out—therefore you should stay on at Wykwyn [the Rutland family estate]—and I can't bear to have you out of my sight. He also admires wholesome animal lust. We'll be married just as soon as the law allows.

After Mark voices his love for her, Marnie protests "You don't love me. I'm just something you've caught. You think I'm some kind of animal you've trapped." Mark warms to her comparison: "That's right, you are. And I've caught something really wild this time, haven't I? I've tracked you and caught you and by God I'm going to keep you." This moment harkens back to an earlier conversation in Mark's office in which he told Marnie about Sophie, the jaguarundi that he tamed and taught to trust him; we imagine that, for Mark, marriage to Marnie constitutes a similar taming project. Subsequently, after Mark warns Marnie to resist the temptation to steal "the Wkywyn silver," pointing out that it will soon be hers by way of marriage, she draws an analogy between her future ownership of the family tableware and the legal possession he will take of her once they wed. Once again, Mark accepts the analogy, then states that "Somebody's got to take on the responsibility for you, Marnie. And it narrows down to a choice of me or the police, old girl." The scene fades out on Marnie, writhing in anguish at the thought of marriage to Mark. Next, we find ourselves at Wykwyn in the immediate aftermath of Marnie and Mark's wedding.

Most noteworthy in the exchange in the car is Mark's framing of marriage in terms of property and the capture and domestication of a wild animal, both key themes in *The Taming of the Shrew*; left unsaid by Mark is the fact that, in the name of his love for her, he is effectively blackmailing Marnie ("me or the police, old girl"). At the same time, he alludes to "tak[ing] on the responsibility" for Marnie. In this scene, Mark's responsibility for Marnie is largely synonymous with his self-perceived ownership of her. At other moments in the film, though, that feeling of responsibility is congruent with Mark's sincere efforts to identify the root causes of Marnie's childhood trauma. In this way, Mark's responsibility-taking encompasses both his commendable and his morally dubious treatment of Marnie—treatment that attests to the film's depiction of the morally conflicted and problematic nature of patriarchal authority.

This scene offers an obvious point of comparison with the central narrative of *The Taming of the Shrew*. At the beginning of that play, Petruccio has set out from Verona to seek his fortune, which he intends to acquire by way of marriage: "I have thrust myself into this maze, / Haply to wive and thrive as best I may."[10] Upon arriving in Padua, he learns about Katherina, the headstrong, violent eldest daughter of Baptista Minola who, her father insists, must be married off before her widely admired, seemingly dutiful younger sister Bianca can be. Through trickery and force of will, Petruccio weds the resistant Katherina and, after the ceremony, he embarks upon the process of "tam[ing] a shrew," whereby he seeks to "curb her mad and headstrong humor" (4.1.190-91). The success of this process is demonstrated in the play's final scene, in which Katherina—or, as Petruccio calls her, Kate—performs her dutifulness, most notably in a final speech directed toward other newly married women.[11] In this speech, Kate focuses on the folly of a wife's disobedience toward the husband who "cares for thee, / And for thy maintenance commits his body / To painful labor both by sea and land . . ." (5.2.147-49). The play ends, then, with Kate publicly acknowledging that Petruccio has, in Mark Rutland's phrase, "take[n] on the responsibility" for her.

To read the play as George Kaplan might, with an eye for evidence of Shakespeare's "healthy concept of normality," is to find in its conclusion a comforting reassertion of the patriarchal status quo. And yet, Shakespeare presents us with a few reasons to question the legitimacy of this ending. For one thing, the *nature* of Kate's transformation isn't entirely clear: has she really become a dutiful wife, or does she temporarily take on that role in the final scenes of the play to get what she wants?[12] This includes besting her ostensibly obedient sister, Bianca, in front of their father: unlike Kate, Bianca fails to come when her husband calls for her, and both he and her father lose a bet as a result of her recalcitrance. For another thing, both the *means* by which Kate is transformed and the *cost* of that transformation, whether it is real or not, are troubling. As Lynda Boose puts it regarding the latter point, "For romantic comedy to 'work' normatively in *Shrew*'s concluding scene and allow the audience the happy ending it demands, the cost is, simply put, the construction of a woman's speech that must unspeak its own resistance and reconstitute female subjectivity into the self-abnegating rhetoric of Kate's famous disquisition on obedience."[13] To put it another way, for some the gap between the compliant Kate of play's end and the Katherina whose verbal sparring with Petruccio before their marriage is a source of comic pleasure is great enough as to be disquieting. Similarly, her praise for a husband who cares for and maintains his wife jars with Petruccio's earlier mistreatment of her.

As for the *means* of Kate's transformation, they have been the subject of much scholarly discussion. Critics have debated the degree of cruelty in Petruccio's method for "taming" her upon their marriage. Before turning to that debate, though, we need to describe his method. The taming process can be said to occur in two main phases, the first occurring on Katherina and Petruccio's wedding day, and the second once they have returned to his home. In the first phase, Petruccio shames Katherina by arriving both late and inebriated to their wedding; by wearing outlandish, inappropriate clothing; and by disrupting the ceremony itself with his bad behavior (among other things, he "[gave the priest] such a cuff / That down fell priest and book" [3.2.157-158]).

Petruccio's tardiness alone is experienced by Katherina as a source of shame—"Now must the world point at poor Katherine . . ." (3.2.18)—and his actions during the ceremony only increase her sense of mortification.[14] However, Petruccio's dubious conduct extends beyond the embarrassing actions discussed here.

After the conclusion of the wedding service, Petruccio insists upon leaving for his home immediately, dragging Kate from her own wedding banquet before it even properly commences.[15] When both she and others try to dissuade Petruccio from this course of action, he treats their resistance as an attempted theft; laying claim to Kate as his property, Petruccio pledges to defend its/her seizure from all comers:

> I will be master of what is mine own.
> She is my goods, my chattels; she is my house,
> My household stuff, my field, my barn,
> My horse, my ox, my ass, my anything,
> And here she stands, touch her whoever dare.
> I'll bring mine action on the proudest he
> That stops my way in Padua. (3.2.222-28)

Petruccio's overreaction to entreaties that his wife be allowed to stay at her own wedding feast often plays as very comical. Even so, his statement of ownership is startling. Significantly, it gestures toward a key concept within early modern thinking about marriage and property ownership. The doctrine of "coverture" granted to a husband the rights to his wife's property. As the historian Keith Wrightson describes it,

> The rights of a married woman, or "femme covert," were seriously curtailed [within that doctrine]. Though a wife retained her title to any freehold lands of her own (unless these were formally transferred), her husband acquired a life interest in the rents and profits of her lands even if she predeceased him, provided there was "live issue" of the marriage. In addition, all her moveable goods and chattels became his.[16]

Insofar as early modern property law places a wife's economic assets in her husband's hands, it invites us to think, as Petruccio does, of the wife herself as property.[17] Moreover, the doctrine of coverture harmonizes with a pervasive conception of marriage, derived from Genesis, that holds man and wife are one being, and that, in terms of his cultural authority, the husband is that being. In a different Shakespeare play, Hamlet plays upon and upends this idea when he refers to Claudius as his mother: "father and mother is man and wife, / Man and wife is one flesh, so [you are] my mother."[18]

Phase two of Petruccio's taming of his wife occurs within his home. Simply put, it entails denying Kate things she needs, including food and sleep, as well as things she wants—new clothes, a trip home—all in the name of taking "reverend care" of his wife. In a famous soliloquy, Petruccio articulates his strategy:

> She ate no meat today, nor none shall eat;
> Last night she slept not, nor tonight she shall not.
> As with the meat, some undeservèd fault
> I'll find about the making of the bed,
> And here I'll fling the pillow, there the bolster,
> This way the coverlet, another way the sheets.
> Ay, and amid this hurly I intend
> That all is done in reverend care of her. (4.1.178-185)

Significantly, Petruccio frames his treatment of Kate in terms of the training of a wild hawk: "My falcon now is sharp and passing empty" (4.1.171). Moreover, this soliloquy concludes with four lines in which Petruccio's analogizing slides from raptor training to shrew taming: "This is a way to kill a wife with kindness, / And thus I'll curb her mad and headstrong humor. / He that knows better how to tame a shrew, / Now let him speak" (4.1.189-192).

As measured by Kate's final speech, Petruccio's taming efforts are successful. The turning point occurs when Kate capitulates to Petruccio's insistence that the sun is the moon, and that an old man they meet on the road is a virginal young woman. The obvious question, of course, is whether Kate's capitulation is sincere—suggesting that Petruccio's mistreatment of her has broken her spirit and rendered her entirely pliant to his will—or whether she plays along with Petruccio's wishes in order to get what she wants (in this instance, a trip back to her father's house in Padua).[19] In the latter case, it becomes possible to see Kate in her final speech as asserting her own agency under the guise of being the thoroughly dutiful, subordinate wife. Through her behavior in the final scene, Kate bests Bianca, whose elopement represents a violence done to patriarchal authority, albeit one that is belatedly condoned; Kate also transforms her father's sense of her: "For she is changed as she had never been [i.e., as if she had never been shrewish]" (5.2.115). And yet, her "taming" has its limitations and its costs, as Judith Haber observes: "It is thus suggested, from one perspective, that, by following Petruccio's orders, Kate gets full command of her voice. . . . But (to reverse the emphasis, as many critics do) we should also note that Kate can play only at Petruccio's direction and that her playfulness ends by paradoxically supporting his control."[20] Moreover, the issue of her cruel mistreatment at her husband's hands lingers in the minds of readers and playgoers.

While most scholars acknowledge the severity of Petruccio's treatment of his wife, many also note its *comparatively* benign nature when viewed historically. Frances E. Dolan and others have shown how the play deviates from other period representations of shrew-taming by *not* depicting a husband who subjects his wife to physical violence; Emily Detmer situates the play in relation to growing cultural resistance to the practice of wife-beating, arguing that "*The Taming of the Shrew* acts as a comedic roadmap for reconfiguring . . . emergent modes of 'skillful' and civilized dominance for *gentle*men, that is, for subordinating a wife without resorting to the 'common' man's brute strength"; and Elizabeth Mathie contends that "codes of gentleness and cruelty within prescriptions for animal training itself can inform our reading of Petruchio's taming."[21] To be clear, these critics are not *exonerating* Petruccio's behavior but *historicizing* it. Moreover, they recognize the difficult ethical position that behavior places audience members in. As Detmer observes, "To enjoy the comedy of the play, readers and viewers must work to see domestic violence from the point of view of an abuser—that is, they must minimalize the violence and, at the same time, justify its use."[22]

One possible, and partial, justification for Petruccio's acts of domestic violence suggests another affinity with Hitchcock's film. As I mentioned above, Petruccio intends to "curb [Kate's] mad and headstrong *humor.*" Petruccio is referencing here Galenic humoral theory. This theory, which is classical in origin but was still current in the sixteenth century, contends that good physical and psychological health derives from maintaining the balance of the four bodily humors: blood, phlegm, choler and black bile. In the telling of Petruccio and various other characters, Katherina's irascible unruliness is attributable to a preponderance of choler; her body's humoral "complexion" or temperament informs her psychological make-up. Moreover, as Gail Kern Paster has shown, Petruccio's taming project can be understood as an effort to transform that complexion through "an active intervention in her body's relation to its environment."[23] Petruccio and his servant Grumio withhold meat from Kate on the grounds that it will feed her choler; her husband denies her sleep in an effort to subdue her to his authority.[24] Read in this way, such actions can be seen as efforts to bring Kate's humoral complexion into balance; and her final statement of compliance to patriarchal authority could appear to be commensurate with the attainment of that balance. Now, there are reasons to qualify such an argument, some of which have already been adduced (e.g., the cruelty inherent in Petruccio's "reverend care" for his wife). Moreover, Kate's choler is mirrored by Petruccio's; if he does not undergo a dramatic humoral transformation, one reason is that he needs to be choleric to some unspecified degree in order to maintain authority over this wife.[25] This double standard is registered in the play without being forcefully contested. As Paster puts it,

"The play does seem to offer an overall endorsement of Kate's taming and assigns Petruchio the task of undertaking it as the crux of his own masculinization."[26] And yet, especially from a modern perspective, this endorsement is shadowed by the severity of Petruccio's efforts to "kill [his] wife with kindness."

*   *   *   *   *   *

In taking up *The Taming of the Shrew* as I have over the last several pages, I have suggested some reasons why Hitchcock detected an affinity between that play and his film. What if we were to reverse the direction of interpretive travel, though? What might be said about Petruccio's motives and methods if we examine them through the lens of *Marnie*—or, more specifically, of Mark's entwined efforts to cure and assert his authority over the film's title character? We have seen Petruccio and Mark claim their spouses as their property—the former just after the wedding service and the latter shortly before it—while also "tak[ing] on the responsibility" for them. How might Mark's taming project inform the way in which we view Petruccio's?

The first, obvious thing to note is that, when considering the nature of Marnie's cure, the psychological coordinates are Freudian rather than Galenic. As Tony Lee Moral has emphasized, both Hitchcock's *Marnie* and Winston Graham's before it partake of the broader "absorption of psychoanalysis into literature, film, and theater" that had been ongoing since the early twentieth-century.[27] Of course, this is true of Hitchcock's works more generally, with films such as *Spellbound* (1945), *Psycho,* and *Vertigo* (1958) displaying an apparent interest in what Jonathan Freedman terms therapeutic culture. Freedman argues that Hitchcock, with *Vertigo*, betrays a profound skepticism about the curative potential of psychoanalysis.[28] Such skepticism is not as clearly on display in *Marnie*, insofar as the title character, Michele Piso observes, "is brought to a breakthrough by a man who helps her confront her past and unlock the repressed truth. . . . On this level, the filmic text projects a therapeutic resolution of social and psychological conflicts."[29] And yet, as is suggested in the car scene discussed earlier, Mark's actions are driven by a twin desire to cure Marnie and to dominate her, sexually and otherwise. In other words, if *Marnie* reveals skepticism about psychoanalysis, that skepticism focuses less on the legitimacy of the cure than on the motives and methods of the amateur analyst, Mark Rutland. To put it another way, the film presents Mark as well as Marnie as suitable subjects for psychological analysis.[30]

Relevant to this issue are the circumstances behind Marnie's hiring by Rutland and Company. Mark insists that, despite the absence of references, Marnie be hired over a more qualified candidate. He does this suspecting that "Mary Taylor" is the same woman who, as Marian Holland, robbed Strutt and Company. While physical attraction undoubtedly plays a role in Mark's demand, so, presumably, does the prospect that Marnie might attempt to rob Rutland and Company—a prospect that would provide Mark with a perverse form of pleasure. In describing to François Truffaut why he chose to turn Graham's novel into a film, Hitchcock alludes to "The fetish idea. A man wants to go to bed with a thief because she is a thief."[31] When Truffaut follows up by asking what draws Mark to Marnie, Hitchcock agrees with both of the French director's suggestions: that Marnie is dependent upon Mark because "he knows her secret" and that "he finds it exciting to go to bed with a thief." In describing what he terms his failure to translate the "fetish idea" to the screen, Hitchcock states that "we'd have had to have Sean Connery catching the girl robbing the safe and show that he felt like jumping at her and raping her on the spot." The second Rutland robbery, with its representation of a physical struggle between Mark and Marnie in which the former dominates the latter, carries us closer to that imagined rape scene than is usually recognized; indeed, the violent conflict we might expect from the film's actual scene of unwanted sexual intercourse is displaced onto the struggle next to the safe.[32] In this particular way, Hitchcock's "fetish idea" lives on in his depiction of the thwarted robbery.

In *Marnie*, then, Hitchcock reveals Mark's taming project, animated by both sincere concern for Marnie and a desire to dominate her, is also bound up with his fetish. The notion that there might be a pathological sexual dimension to Petruccio's taming of Kate has been underexplored in criticism on *The Taming of the Shrew*.[33] One reason for this is that, in his "kill a wife with kindness" soliloquy, Petruccio's taming strategy is strikingly devoid of overt sexual content. Crucial to our analysis of that speech is the fact that it describes the newlywed couple's behavior on their wedding night. In the place of the marriage's sexual consummation, we are presented with scenes of privation: the withholding from Kate of food first and then sleep. Sex is evoked in its absence. Petruccio notes that, come bedtime, he will "fling [here] the pillow, there the bolster, / This way the coverlet, another way the sheets." Where we might expect the bedclothes to be scattered as a result of amorous activity, we instead find them tossed aside by Petruccio to deny Kate any rest. To put it another way, Petruccio seeks to assert his mastery over his new wife not through sexual means, but by expunging sexuality along with sleep from their wedding night. In this way, his actions are marked by a degree of self-restraint that might seem to suggest an attenuated sexual desire—or, indeed, to imply there is a vacuum where we would expect such a desire to exist.[34]

But what if, under the influence of *Marnie*, we were to view Petruccio's actions as having a pathological dimension? As Shirley Nelson Garner has noted, Kate's "humiliation has a sexually sadistic tinge since there is always the possibility that Petruchio will rape her, as he threatens earlier: 'For I will board her, though she chide as loud / As thunder when the clouds in autumn crack' [1.2.93-94]."[35] That threat notwithstanding, Petruccio does not rape Kate, and the consummation of their marriage is deferred until after the end of the play—after, that is, Kate pledges her obeisance to Petruccio and he bests the other husbands through his wife's performance of fealty. Crucially, that performance culminates in a potent ritual of subordination: Kate offers to place her hands under her husband's foot "in token of [her] duty" (5.2.178). As Lynda Boose has noted, this gesture evokes an "adamantly hierarchical and patriarchal . . . form of the [English] wedding service" that had been superseded by the time of the play.[36] As such, the gesture can be seen to have a broader narrative and symbolic function: if Katherina and Petruccio's wedding was marred by his taming efforts, here we encounter a brief reprise of that ceremony marked by the couple's newfound harmony. The implication, moreover, is that only now will the marriage be consummated, as is suggested when Petruccio says "Come, Kate, we'll to bed" (5.2.184). Seen in this light, Kate's willingness to place her body at and under Petruccio's feet is a precondition for, and perhaps the engine of, his sexual pleasure.

Despite the threat mentioned in the preceding paragraph, Petruccio does not sexually assault Kate; he does, however, at one point treat her as his property in a way that evokes the doctrine of coverture ("She is my goods, my chattels," etc.). That doctrine had crucial implications for the way in which rape was conceptualized in the early modern period. As a glance at the *Oxford English Dictionary* will remind us, the oldest meaning of "rape," dating to the fourteenth century and still current in the sixteenth, is "The act of taking something by force; *esp.* the seizure of property by violent means" (*OED*, "rape," noun[3] 1). This definition casts an interesting light on Petruccio's speech about the supposed efforts of various weddinggoers to abduct Kate and thus prevent her from traveling home with him: he is accusing them of rape. To the more familiar definition of the word as "the act or crime, committed by a man, of forcing a woman to have sexual intercourse with him against her will" (2a), the *OED* appends this note: "Historically, rape was considered to be the act of a man forcing a woman other than his wife to have intercourse against her will." Taken together, Petruccio's speech and these *OED* definitions illustrate the point made by Barbara J. Baines in relation to Shakespeare's *The Rape of Lucrece*: early modern legal discourse treats rape as a crime of property.[37] Moreover, insofar as his wife was understood as a man's property, rape within marriage was deemed a legal impossibility. Rape could only involve "a man forcing a woman *other than his wife*" — and even in that instance, the transgression was against the husband, not his wife (who, after all, was conceived of as either an extension of him or his property). Seen in this light, it is not merely that Petruccio doesn't rape Kate; it is that, as her husband, he couldn't legally be understood to do so.

Which brings us back to *Marnie*. Scholars have debated whether or not we should understand Mark's sexual encounter with Marnie on the ship as rape.[38] While in my view Mark clearly commits an act of non-consensual sexual intercourse, it is worth noting that Mark is not technically guilty of the crime of rape.[39] (Of course, the film is not primarily concerned with technical guilt, but with the implications of this act for each of the characters and their relationship.) This is because, at the time that the movie was made and released, marital rape was an impossibility within the law. Writing in 1957, Rollin M. Perkins, author of a widely used textbook on criminal law, asserts that "A man does not commit rape by having sexual intercourse with his lawful wife, even if he does so by force and against her will."[40] Perkins is making a complacent allusion to the "marital rape exception," which derives its authority from what was known as the Lord Hale doctrine. An English chief justice, Sir Matthew Hale contended in 1736 that "the husband cannot be guilty of a rape committed by himself upon his lawful wife, for by their mutual matrimonial consent and contract the wife hath given up herself in this kind unto her husband, which she cannot retract."[41] Undergirding this view is the doctrine of coverture. Rebecca M. Ryan's discussion of that doctrine's application in eighteenth- and nineteenth-century legal thought includes unintentional echoes of Kate's final speech in *The Taming of the Shrew*:

> Under coverture, the wife forfeited her legal existence, thereby forfeiting her independent rights in the law; the husband assumed her rights, or assumed right over

her; in return, he was to offer the protection she presumably required in her weakened state. If his duty was protection, her duty was, above all else, obedience. Nineteenth-century legal scholar James Schouler wrote: "It is for the wife to love, honor, and obey: it is for the husband to love, cherish, and protect."[42]

As Ryan and others have shown, the marital rape exception persisted for a variety of reasons, including a reluctance to intervene in the domestic sphere and a failure to take spousal abuse, sexual or otherwise, seriously enough. In the U.S. today, while marital rape is illegal, there are loopholes in a number of states that allow it to be punished less severely than its non-marital counterpart.[43] Such loopholes offer evidence of the continued downplaying, at least within the legal arena, of marital rape's severity and significance.

I have suggested that the violence of Mark's shipboard sexual assault is displaced onto the scene in which Marnie attempts to rob the Rutland and Company safe for a second time. Within that scene, Marnie finds herself unable to remove money from that safe, even as Mark exhorts her to do so—"What's mine belongs to you. It's yours. You're not stealing"—and even forces her hand toward the stacks of bills. Mark's line brings to mind his earlier exhortation to Marnie that she not steal "the Wkywyn silver" before they marry because it will become hers after they do so. In both instances, Mark evokes the conception of marital unity, but the promise of functional equality within marriage—what's mine is yours—is belied by the physical force Mark expends in trying to bend Marnie to his will (and, of course, by his blackmailing her into marriage in the first place). As for other reasons why Marnie is unexpectedly resistant to taking the money, they emerge out of the untenable position in which she finds herself. She is simultaneously Mark's property (as they discuss in the car, he takes legal possession of her when they wed), putative co-owner of his property (what is his is hers), and would-be thief of that property.[44] This scene foregrounds for both Marnie and us the impossibility of that position, which she has occupied since the wedding. If in the wake of the thwarted robbery Marnie relinquishes her status as thief, what is left to be resolved—beyond, of course, the nature of her childhood trauma—is whether Marnie comes to experience her marriage to Mark in terms of marital unity or of legal possession.

While Hitchcock's "fetish idea" lives on in the second Rutland robbery scene, the thwarted theft has an erotic dimension for Marnie as well as Mark, at least initially. As Joe McElhaney has observed, Marnie "derives a displaced sexual thrill from her thefts [that] is made explicit . . . when . . . she attempts to rob the safe again with a look on her face approaching sexual bliss as she, in a low angle shot, slowly and lovingly turns the knob on the safe door."[45] The question of Marnie's sexuality has long intrigued commentators on the film. If Hitchcock himself referred to Marnie as "basically frigid," Robert J. Corber sees her as being coded as a femme lesbian, while David Greven locates what he terms Marnie's "queer resilience" in a "sexuality [that] is open-ended and does not conform to one sexual mode."[46] The conclusion of the film might seem to suggest that the open-endedness of Marnie's sexuality gives way to a conventional heterosexual attachment to her husband—this, after all, is part of the promise of Marnie's "cure," that through confronting her childhood trauma she will grow able, in Mark's phrase, to "stand to have a man touch her."[47] And yet, the film ends in a fashion that suggests this promise has not—or at least not yet—been realized, as Marnie tells Mark, "I don't want to go to jail. I'd rather stay with you." This does not read as a sincere expression of Marnie's love for Mark or even a full-throated endorsement of married life. Rather, marriage to and sex with Mark can plausibly be construed as the better of two bad options—just as Kate's acts of obeisance at the end of *The Taming of the Shrew* could be interpreted as making the best of a circumstance in which her agency has been radically circumscribed.[48]

What about the question of Kate's sexuality? It should first be observed that Katherina diverges from the early modern stereotype of the unruly, shrewish woman in one crucial way. As

Valerie Traub observes, "The ideology of chastity, constraints against female speech, and women's confinement within the domestic household are summed up by the phrase 'the body enclosed,' which refers simultaneously to a woman's closed genitals, closed mouth, and her enclosure within the home."[49] To put it in terms of a period commonplace, the ideal woman is "chaste, silent, and obedient," with the understanding that a deviation from that ideal in one of these three arenas of behavior signals a deviation in all three.[50] To put it simply, female volubility and disobedience were understood to be close companions to female promiscuity. What is distinctive about Katherina, then, is that while she is neither silent nor obedient, her chastity is never in doubt. Additionally, her "shrewish" violent behavior toward men does not connote a resistance to matrimony in general. We have seen that she feels mortified by Petruccio's behavior on their wedding day; earlier in the play, she bemoans the fact that Bianca, whom she believes to be her father's favorite, will have a husband while she is destined to "lead apes in hell," the proverbial fate of women who do not marry (2.1.34). That being said, the question of Kate's sexual desire is not one that the play brings up.[51] Unlike Juliet, Kate does not soliloquize about her impatient longing for her husband to come to her on their wedding night; nor are we granted anything like Portia's lovesick urgings to Bassanio in The Merchant of Venice that he postpone choosing a casket for fear he will select the wrong one and be expelled from her life; nor, indeed, do we encounter, as in As You Like It or A Midsummer Night's Dream, any intimations of a former same-sex amorous attachment.[52] Instead of articulations of desire, we have first Kate's resistance to Petruccio, then later her expression of fealty to him. If The Taming of the Shrew makes room for Petruccio's fetish, it does not create a space for Kate's sexual desires—except, perhaps, insofar as they have become entirely congruent with her husband's. Does Kate make the best of a bad situation, then, or does she, unlike Marnie, find sexual satisfaction in the role she previously spurned? The latter possibility would offer one explanation for her apparent eagerness to place her hands beneath Petruccio's foot.

*   *   *   *   *   *

In discussing the combination of violence, possessiveness, sexual fetishism, and "reverend care" observable in Petruccio and Mark's actions toward their respective spouses, I have suggested that both Shakespeare and Hitchcock raise pressing questions about the nature and limits of patriarchal authority, especially as that authority is expressed in the doctrine of coverture and in rape laws. In concluding, I want to redirect our attention slightly, from patriarchal authority to the place of fathers in these two works. Let us return to the exchange between Mark and Marnie with which my analysis of the film began. In the midst of articulating his plan to marry Marnie, Mark twice alludes to the fact that his father will approve of his intentions: "That'll please Dad, he admires action"; and "He also admires wholesome animal lust." Upon their return from their aborted honeymoon, Mark informs his new bride that his morning routine always involves breakfast with his father—and, of course, it is with his father (and, after they marry, also with Marnie and his sister-in-law Lil) that he lives at Wykwyn. In all of these ways, Mark is noticeably solicitous of Dad's opinions, feelings, and routines. At the same time, as Deborah Thomas has astutely argued, Mark has ample reason to resent the man

> whose refusal to set foot inside Rutland's doesn't prevent him from taking pleasure in a leisured life of elegance that the company profits make possible. His comment when Mark brings Marnie to the house for the first time— "It bewilders me what any of you can find to do at Rutland's"—adds insult to injury and underlines his aristocratic mentality in refraining from dirtying his hands with work, while nonetheless enjoying the fruits of the labors of others, most particularly his son.[53]

Moreover, the film makes clear that Mark's professional ambitions were zoological, and that he stepped in to run Rutland and Company only in order to keep it afloat. One reason he did so was to support his father, who, as Thomas observes, seems notably unappreciative. Additionally, Mark's disdain for both riding horses and hunting, favorite pastimes of his father's, is designed to signal a degree of rebelliousness toward him and his milieu. The main point is that, in Mark's ambivalent relationship to Dad, we can see why his fetish takes the form it does, combining the impulse to wound the company that bears his father's name with the desire to save it. In figuratively saving the company by thwarting Marnie and then facilitating her cure, Mark can be seen as overcoming that impulse. We might also speculate that he reconciles himself to the world that he has long inhabited but held at a distance. And, in his view, his very marriage to Marnie was bound to win his father's approbation, even when saving the company did not.[54]

As for Petruccio, I have mentioned his ambition to "wive and thrive." Significantly, his pursuit of that objective has a precipitating event: "Antonio, my father, is deceased, / And I have thrust myself into this maze, / Haply to wive and thrive as best I may" (1.2.52-54). One might assume that Petruccio seeks to wed because, in the wake of his father's death, he lacks resources. However, as becomes plain during the negotiations over Katherina's dowry, he has inherited a good deal of wealth, which he in turn has "bettered rather than decreased" (see 2.1.118). Moreover, the case he makes for himself to Baptista hinges upon the fact that Baptista "knew my father well *and in him me*" (2.1.116; my emphasis). The knowledge Petruccio alludes to here is grounded in reputation, not personal experience.[55] It is by way of reputation, then, that a patriarchal network is extended, as one man's son is proven viable as another's son-in-law.[56] Importantly, Petruccio is very keen on becoming a part of that network. Immediately after discussing the terms of the dowry, he refers to Baptista as "father" (2.1.130), and this is only the first time he identifies him as such; he later describes Baptista to Kate as "*our* fathe[r]" (4.6.1; my emphasis), and in the subsequent scene he mentions going to "*My* father's [house]" (5.1.9; my emphasis). To put it simply, Petruccio's trajectory is

from a single, fatherless state to a married one marked for him
by the formation of new paternal relationships. Whereas
Mark's relationship to his father is, at least until the end of the
film, defined by ambivalence, Petruccio's search for a wife
carries with it the promise of acquiring a new father. Both
characters are at the end of their respective stories more firmly
ensconced within the world of their fathers. At the same time,
in outstripping Mr. Rutland and Baptista Minola—Mark by
saving the company, and Petruccio by taming Kate—these
men prove themselves to be capable future patriarchs. They
arguably do so, however, at some expense to their wives and
in pursuit of non-normative sexual desires. To put it another
way, in both *The Taming of the Shrew* and *Marnie* the oppressive
dimensions of "normality" are exposed even as normality
itself is at least superficially affirmed.

*   *   *   *   *   *

Earlier, I made the obvious point that *Marnie* is not an
adaptation of *The Taming of the Shrew*. However, this essay's
analysis resonates with "the oldest meaning of the noun
'adaptation': "the action of applying one thing to another or
bringing two things together so as to effect a change in the nature
of the objects." As Kamilla Elliott notes, this definition, which
(like *The Taming of the Shrew*) derives from the late sixteenth
century, implies "mutual, *reciprocal* change."[57] I have tried to
suggest that, when placed by Hitchcock in dialogue with one
another, these two works are changed and, by extension, our
sense of what counts as "Hitchcockian" or "Shakespearean" is
also expanded. Tracing particular alterations does not require
that we ignore the historical specificity of these works; instead,
it helps to deepen the conversation, to sharpen our
understanding of the modifications these texts undergo when
we place them in relation to one another. If it is imprecise to say
that *Marnie* "was" *The Taming of the Shrew*, it is generative to treat
it as an adaptation in the sense described here; and, by so doing,
to chart the "mutual, reciprocal" changes the film and play
undergo when we accept Hitchcock's invitation to equate them.

In developing this argument, I have offered historical contextualization for certain elements of *Marnie* and *The Taming of the Shrew*—a process that, perhaps surprisingly, reveals a degree of continuity between the sixteenth and twentieth centuries when it comes to coverture, marital unity, and marital rape. Of course, there are features of the works and their historical moments that I have not explored; nor have I considered ways in which similarities between *Marnie* and *The Taming of the Shrew* might conceal important formal, narrative or ideological differences between them. (For instance, *The Taming of the Shrew* is typical of many Shakespeare plays in erasing mothers, and maternal influence, from the scene; whereas *Marnie*, like *Psycho*, *Notorious* (1946), *The Birds* (1963), and others, is centrally concerned with mothers and their impacts on their children.). My objective has been to follow Hitchcock's lead by putting his film in dialogue with Shakespeare's play, and, in so doing, to offer a more expansive conception of what might count as "Hitchcockian" or "Shakespearean." It seems certain that, unlike George Kaplan, Hitchcock did not locate within *The Taming of the Shrew* evidence of Shakespeare's status as the poet of healthy normality; instead, the play provides him with ample occasion for identifying "Hitchcockian" elements within it. As such, *The Taming of the Shrew* licenses us to consider not only what Hitchcock sees in Shakespeare, but also where Shakespeare and Hitchcock find common ground.

Notes

I would like to thank Greg Semenza, Sidney Gottlieb, and Deborah Thomas for their invaluable feedback on this essay.

1. George Kaplan, "Alfred Hitchcock: Lost in the Wood," *Film Comment* 8 (November-December 1972): 47. Henceforth cited in text by page number only.
2. Robin Wood, *Hitchcock's Films Revisited*, rev. ed. (New York: Columbia University Press, 2002).
3. Wood, *Hitchcock's Films Revisited*, 57-58.

4. Wood, *Hitchcock's Films Revisited*, 65. Later, he compares the film, along with *Vertigo* (1958), *Psycho* (1960), and *The Birds* (1963), to "the mature tragedies of Shakespeare" (197).

5. Wood, *Hitchcock's Films Revisited*, xiv.

6. For discussions of connections between the two artists, see Sidney Gottlieb, "Hitchcock and Shakespeare," online at https://blog.oup.com/2017/08/hitchcock-and-shakespeare; Tony Howard, "Mr. Hitchcock's Shakespeare," *Around the Globe: The Magazine of Shakespeare's Globe* (1999): 33; Wendy Lesser, "Hitchcock and Shakespeare," *Threepenny Review* 11 (Autumn 1982): 17-19.

7. Charlotte Chandler, *It's Only a Movie: Alfred Hitchcock, A Personal Biography* (New York: Simon and Schuster, 2005), 273.

8. See, for example, William Rothman, *Hitchcock: The Murderous Gaze*, 2nd ed. (Albany: State University of New York, 2012), 379.

9. Winston Graham, *Marnie* (rpt. London: Pan Books, 2013).

10. William Shakespeare, *The Taming of the Shrew*, *The Norton Shakespeare: Essential Plays and The Sonnets*, ed. Stephen Greenblatt, et al. (New York: W.W. Norton, 2016), 1.2.53-54. Henceforth cited in text. I have adopted this edition's spelling of this character's name, which frequently appears in other editions as Petruchio. I have not modified the spelling when the name appears as such in critical quotations.

11. For reasons having to do with the relationship between marriage and property discussed later in this essay, I distinguish unwed "Katherina" from wedded "Kate" by way of these different names. I have not modified quotations from other critics to accord with this distinction.

12. On the notion that Kate's final speech is a performance, see, among others, Amy L. Smith, "Performing Marriage with a Difference: Wooing, Wedding, and Bedding in *The Taming of the Shrew*," *Comparative Drama* 36, nos. 3 and 4 (2002): 289-320; Holly A. Crocker, "Affective Resistance: Performing Passivity and Playing A-Part in *The Taming of the Shrew*," *Shakespeare Quarterly* 54 (2003): 142-59; and Elizabeth Mathie, "Critiquing Mastery and Maintaining Hierarchy in *The Taming of the Shrew*," *Studies in English Literature* 60 (2020): 257-76.

13. Lynda E. Boose, "Scolding Brides and Bridling Scolds: Taming the Woman's Unruly Member," *Shakespeare Quarterly* 42, no. 2 (Summer, 1991), 179.

14. She also asks "[W]hat mockery will it be / To want the bridegroom when the priest attends / To speak the ceremonial rites of marriage?" (3.2.4-6).

15. Ann C. Christensen argues that "In removing her from the public feast at Padua and in forbidding her the commanding private position at home, Petruchio not only denies Katherine material sustenance and social identity; he also divests her of the social status and recognition due a mistress" ("Of Household Stuff and Homes: The Stage and Social Practice in *The Taming of the Shrew*," *Explorations in Renaissance Culture* 22 [1996], 133).

16. Keith Wrightson, *Earthly Necessities: Economic Lives in Early Modern Britain* (New Haven: Yale University Press, 2000), 43. As Wrightson acknowledges, there was some regional variability when it came to women's property rights within marriage, but coverture was the dominant model.

17. It should be noted that prescriptive literature devoted to household management had to navigate a basic contradiction. On the one hand, the husband was preeminent within the domestic arena; on the other, there was often functional equality between husband and wife, especially when it came to supervising children or servants. Marriage was simultaneously a hierarchical and companionate institution. As Wrightson nicely puts it, "In practice, domestic relations were shot through with ambiguities and inconsistencies. Yet the ubiquity of patriarchal assumptions can never be ignored. Moreover, they were firmly embodied in law, most fundamentally in the law of property" (*Earthly Necessities*, 42).

18. *Hamlet, The Norton Shakespeare*, 3.6.48-49.

19. Petruccio is explicit about her capitulation as a precondition for their journey: "It shall be moon, or star, or what I list, / [Before] I journey to your father's house" (4.6.7-8).

20. Judith Haber, "Comedy and Eros: Sexualities on Shakespeare's Stage," *The Oxford Handbook to Shakespearean Comedy*, ed. Heather Hirschfeld (Oxford: Oxford University Press, 2018), 284.

21. Frances E. Dolan, "Household Chastisements: Gender, Authority, and 'Domestic Violence,'" in *Renaissance Culture and the Everyday*, ed. Patricia Fumerton and Simon Hunt (Philadelphia: University of Pennsylvania Press, 1998), 206-07; Emily Detmer, "Civilizing Subordination: Domestic Violence and *The Taming of the Shrew*," *Shakespeare Quarterly* 48, no. 3 (Autumn 1997), 274, emphasis in original; Mathie, "Critiquing Mastery and Maintaining Hierarchy in *The Taming of the Shrew*," 258. See also Boose, "Scolding Brides"; Natasha Korda, "Household Kates: Domesticating Commodities in *The Taming of the Shrew*," *Shakespeare Quarterly* 47, no. 2 (Summer 1996), 109.

22. Detmer, "Civilizing Subordination," 274. See also Shirley Nelson Garner, *"The Taming of the Shrew*: Inside or Outside of the Joke?," *"Bad" Shakespeare: Revaluations of the Shakespeare Canon*, ed. Maurice Charney (Rutherford: Fairleigh Dickinson University Press, 1988), 106.

23. Gail Kern Paster, *Humoring the Body: Emotions and the Shakespearean Stage* (Chicago: University of Chicago Press, 2004), 88.

24. David B. Goldstein points out that Galen himself argued against this course of action on the grounds that fasting breeds choler ("Homeschooling the Girl Stomach," *The Taming of the Shrew: The State of Play*, ed. Heather C. Easterling and Jennifer Flaherty [London: The Arden Shakespeare, 2021], 46). Paster makes clear that Petruccio's actions should be taken not as normative but as part of a "humoral fantasy" of the radical transformation of an unruly wife's temperament (88).

25. Paster, *Humoring the Body*, 132. Paster argues that "Petruchio finds a way to make his own choler socially productive by directing it against an even less socialized, even more disruptive object than himself" (130).

26. Paster, *Humoring the Body*, 129. In contrast, Maurice Hunt observes that by "staging anger as a problematic emotional phenomenon, Shakespeare begs the question of whether Katherina's and Petruccio's irascible behavior is finally or only temporarily resolved" (*"The Taming of the Shrew* and Anger," *The Ben Jonson Journal* 27, no. 1 [2020], 106).

27. Tony Lee Moral, *Hitchcock and the Making of* Marnie, rev. ed. (London: The Scarecrow Press, 2013), 7. It is worth noting that contemporary critical appraisals of Hitchcock's film were dismissive of what was perceived to be its simplistic Freudianism; see Robert E. Kapsis, "The Historical Reception of Hitchcock's *Marnie*," *Journal of Film and Video* 40, no. 3 (Summer 1988): 46-63.

28. Jonathan Freedman, "From *Spellbound* to *Vertigo*: Alfred Hitchcock and Therapeutic Culture in America," *Hitchcock's America*, eds. Freedman and Richard Millington (Oxford: Oxford University Press, 1999), 77-98.

29. Michele Piso, "Mark's *Marnie*," *A Hitchcock Reader*, 2nd ed., eds. Marshall Deutelbaum and Leland Poague (Malden, MA: Wiley-Blackwell, 2009), 292. Piso contends that this "Utopian resolution" is undermined by other elements of the film, including the fact that "Mark's capital and aggression are victorious" (292).

30. This is made explicit when Marnie asks Mark to consider his "pathological fix on a woman who . . . screams if you come near her."

31. François Truffaut, with the collaboration of Helen G. Scott, *Hitchcock*, revised ed. (New York: Simon and Schuster, 1984), 301.

32. As Tony Lee Moral observes, "Mark derives cruel pleasure from Marnie's painful entrapment and shows obvious enjoyment when he catches her failed robbery attempt at the safe" (*Hitchcock and the Making of* Marnie, 51). Hitchcock would offer a graphically violent depiction of rape and murder eight years later in *Frenzy* (1972).

33. A significant exception is Barbara Hodgdon, who argued for the sadistic dimensions of Petruccio's actions in relation to pornographic fantasy ("Katherina Bound; Or, Play(K)ating the Strictures of Everyday Life," *PMLA* 107, no. 3 [May 1992], 539).

34. It is worth noting that Petruccio insists from the outset of the play that his only objective in marrying is to accumulate wealth (see 1.2.64-74).

35. Garner, "*The Taming of the Shrew*: Inside or Outside of the Joke?," 114.

36. Lynda E. Boose, "*The Taming of the Shrew*, Good Husbandry, and Enclosure," in *Shakespeare Reread: The Texts in New Contexts*, ed. Russ McDonald (Ithaca: Cornell University Press, 1994), 195.

37. Barbara J. Baines," Effacing Rape in Early Modern Representation," *English Literary History* 65 (1998), 85.

38. Among those who suggest it is not rape—or, at least, that Mark does not intend or view it as such—are Robin Wood (*Hitchcock's Films Revisited*, 394-95), William Rothman (*Hitchcock: The Murderous Gaze*, 411-16), and Murray Pomerance (*Marnie* [Houndmills: Palgrave Macmillan for the British Film Institute, 2014], 33-35). I agree with David Greven that "One of the most perplexing trends in criticism of this film is the effort to exonerate Mark from charges of rape in the shipboard scene in which he forces Marnie, now his wife, to submit to him sexually" (*Intimate Violence: Hitchcock, Sex and Queer Theory* [Oxford: Oxford University Press, 2017], 206). At the same time, as I show above, the *legal* charge of rape is not one that could be applied to Mark at the time of the film's release.

39. Screenwriter Evan Hunter famously resisted the inclusion of this scene in the film on the grounds that the audience would lose all sympathy with Mark. He was replaced by Jay Presson Allen, who had no qualms about the scene. See Moral, *Hitchcock and the Making of* Marnie.

40. Quoted in Rebecca M. Ryan, "The Sex Right: A Legal History of the Marital Rape Exemption," *Law and Social Inquiry* 20, no. 4 (Autumn 1995), 941. See also Jill Elaine Hasday, "Contest and Consent: A Legal History of Marital Rape," *California Law Review* 88 (2000): 1373-1505.

41. Jennifer A. Bennice and Patricia A. Resick, "Marital Rape: History, Research, and Practice," *Trauma, Violence, and Abuse* 4, no. 3 (July 2003), 229.

42. Ryan, "The Sex Right," 944.

43. Rebecca Pirius, "Marital Rape Laws," *Criminal Defense Lawyer*, online at https://www.criminaldefenselawyer.com/marital-rape-laws.html (updated October 12, 2022).

44. Deborah Thomas notes that "her final inability to steal Mark's money and his insistence that the money is legally hers—even if she herself is legally his—are dramatized in front of the open door of the safe at Rutland's, providing a vivid illustration of how limited Marnie's options are." ("Self-Possession and Dispossession in *Marnie*," *Hitchcock Annual* 15 (2006/2007), 119).

45. Joe McElhaney, *The Death of Classical Cinema: Hitchcock, Lang, Minnelli* (Albany: SUNY Press, 2006), 125. See also Greven, *Intimate Violence*, 196.

46. Quoted in Moral, *Hitchcock and the Making of* Marnie, ix; Robert J. Corber, *Cold War Femme: Lesbianism, National Identity, and Hollywood Cinema* (Durham: Duke University Press, 2011), 72-94; Greven, *Intimate Violence*, 191.

47. As Corber shrewdly points out, there is evidence to suggest the change had started to occur earlier in the film: "Marnie no longer resists her role as Mark's wife, but plays the part of a 'society hostess' at a dinner party the night before WykWyn's annual foxhunt. . . . The process of Marnie's incorporation into the institutions of heterosexuality begins *before* Mark forces her to return to her mother's house and relive the sailor's murder" (*Cold War Femme*, 93).

48. Greven reads the ending of the film in this way: "If Marnie gains a 'local' knowledge about her own backstory, she is nevertheless trapped within the social order's resolute commitment to the heterosexualization of all its subjects, and the film allows us to see precisely this" (*Intimate Violence*, 206).

49. Valerie Traub, "Gender and Sexuality in Shakespeare," in *The Cambridge Companion to Shakespeare*, ed. Margreta de Grazia and Stanley Wells (Cambridge: Cambridge University Press, 2006), 131. Traub is drawing on Peter Stallybrass, "Patriarchal Territories: The

Body Enclosed," *Rewriting the Renaissance: The Discourses of Sexual Difference in Early Modern Europe,* ed. Margaret W. Ferguson, Maureen Quilligan, and Nancy Vickers (Chicago: University of Chicago Press, 1986), 123-42.

50. Chastity can refer to either virginity or conjugal loyalty.

51. Relatedly, Ann Blake observes that "unlike other Shakespearean comedies, there is almost no poetic evocation of romantic feeling" in this play ("*The Taming of the Shrew*: Making Fun of Katherine," *The Cambridge Quarterly* 31 [2002], 238).

52. See Traub, "Gender and Sexuality in Shakespeare," 143-44; and Traub, *The Renaissance of Lesbianism in Early Modern England* (Cambridge: Cambridge University Press, 2002), 158-87.

53. Thomas, "Self-Possession and Dispossession in *Marnie*," 118.

54. As someone who has made herself over to appear as a "respectable young woman who can pour tea, ride horses, [and] dress elegantly," Marnie is also well positioned to earn Père Rutland's admiration (Florence Jacobowitz, "Hitchcock and Feminist Criticism: From *Rebecca* to *Marnie*," *A Companion to Alfred Hitchcock*, eds. Thomas Leitch and Leland Poague [Malden, MA: Wiley-Blackwell, 2014], 461).

55. In an earlier example, Petruccio alludes to knowing Baptista, but it is clear he has never met him (1.2.99).

56. The operations of this patriarchal reputational economy are not restricted to Petruccio. The father of Lucentio, the successful suitor of Bianca, "is not all unknown" to Baptista (1.2.238). Interestingly, the operations of this economy are put under comic pressure when an old man identified as Pedant takes on the role of Vincentio, Lucentio's father, and authorizes his "son's" marriage to Bianca.

57. Kamilla Elliott, *Theorizing Adaptation* (Oxford: Oxford University Press, 2020), 33; my emphasis. As Elliott notes, the *OED*'s first example for the definition recorded here dates from 1597.

SUBARNA MONDAL

The Olfactory World of *Alfred Hitchcock's* Psycho

> "Here's the smell of blood still."
> — *Macbeth* (5.1.47)[1]

It has been a conventional assumption that most arts are meant to be seen and heard. Art especially privileges sight. Scholars like Alain Corbin, Constance Classen, and William Ian Miller have explained this tendency of prioritizing the human sense of sight as directly linked to the post-Enlightenment agenda of relegating the sense of smell to the dregs of human experience.[2] Smell is associated with bestiality, insanity, and barbarity. Smell invades. It rules the realm of unreason. As Classen, Howes, and Synnott state in *Aroma: The Cultural History of Smell:*

> The devaluation of smell in the contemporary West is directly linked to the revaluation of the senses which took place during the eighteenth and nineteenth centuries. The philosophers and scientists of that period decided that, while sight was the preeminent sense of reason and civilization, smell was the sense of madness and savagery.[3]

Kant, for example, identifies smell as an antagonist to the highest human values:

> Smell is taste at a distance . . . and others are forced to share the pleasure of it, whether they want to or not. And thus smell is contrary to freedom . . . . Filth seems

to arouse nausea, not so much through what is repugnant to the eyes and tongue as through the stench that we presume it has.[4]

Freud carries this line of thought into the early twentieth century, emphasizing how human progress revolves around leaving behind an attachment to lower bodily functions and senses that link us to them:

> The diminution in importance of olfactory stimuli seems itself, however, to be a consequence of man's erecting himself from the earth . . . Man's' erect posture . . . would represent the beginning of the momentous process of cultural evolution . . . . Dogs . . . incur the contempt of men through two of their characteristics, i.e., that they are creatures of smell and have no horror of excrement.[5]

Recently, however, there has been a countermovement to recuperate what were often disregarded or shunned as lower senses, challenging the dominance of without necessarily abandoning attention to the sense of sight. Olfactory, gustatory, tactile, or auditory senses can come forth, even more powerfully, when read visually. Texts such as written narratives, photographs, and films can be reread for sensory hints. In this essay, I examine Hitchcock's *Psycho* (1960) as a text in which sight works with olfactory perceptions and aids in buttressing the "inter sensoriality" of the film. I attempt to reinterpret many of the visual cues as olfactory ones and examine how they affect the viewer's multi-sensory experience of the film.

Theories of Embodied Spectatorship: A Brief Overview

A recuperation of the importance of the sense of smell is part of a broader movement emphasizing the need to expand our appreciation of the importance of other senses besides sight in perception in general and also in the way art works and is experienced. Maurice Merleau-Ponty's *Phenomenology of Perception* (published in 1945 and translated and published in England in 1962) proved to be an important initial step in the development of critical theories on embodied spectatorship. By addressing the body as a feeling and a perceiving organism, Merleau-Ponty tries to surpass the Cartesian dyad of empiricism and intellectualism that has dominated Western philosophy: "The world is not what I think, but what I live through."[6] Such a theory has a tremendous effect on the notions of cinema spectatorship.

The viewer's body as receiver of on-screen images was given its due importance in the works of early film theorists like Hugo Munsterberg, Vsevolod Pudovkin, and Sergei Eisenstein. In *The Corporeal Image: Film, Ethnography, and the Senses*, David MacDougall traces the idea of embodiment to the days when cinema was in its early stages:

> It is no accident that Eisenstein chose the word "collision" to express the effect of juxtaposing two shots, and it is this concept of dynamic energy that permeates much of his writing on the various forms of montage . . . . At one point he describes the "psycho-physiological" effect of a series of shots of farmers mowing with scythes, causing the audience to rock "from side to side."[7]

MacDougall further states: "Pudovkin, too, suggests that manipulating the editing tempo can affect the viewer physically and emotionally." Thus, the early Soviet filmmakers were enthusiastic about "[discovering] new ways of creating bodily sensations, exploiting the kinesthetic potential of images through camera work."[8]

As traced by Vivian Sobchack, interest in the visceral effects of the cinema reached its height in the 1930s and 1940s with the empirical tests conducted by the Payne Studies in the United States (like checking the blood pressure of the film audience) and the publication of works by Walter Benjamin and Siegfried Kracauer.[9] In "The Work of Art in the Age of Mechanical Reproduction" (1935), Benjamin speaks of filmic understanding in terms of tactile appropriation.[10] Kracauer, on the other hand, attributes the distinctiveness of films to their capability of rousing us sensually. He understands the viewer as a "corporeal-material being," a "human being with skin and hair": "The material elements that present themselves in films directly stimulate the material layers of the human being: his nerves, his senses, his entire physiological substance."[11]

Toward the end of the twentieth century, we witness a growing body of critical theoretical works that, apart from exploring the centrality of the eye and its relation to the self, utilize a whole array of embodied experiences and senses of the audience while interpreting a text. Deleuze and Guattari's ideas on sensation and affect in *Anti-Oedipus* (1972) influenced later theorists at the turn of the twentieth century to explore the myriad corporeal possibilities of film spectatorship. Deleuze's study of neuroscience opened newer avenues in an already rich field of cinema studies. Deleuze's study also seeks to understand the film spectator within what Paul Elliott refers to as the "postmodern scopic regime" — one who is fragmented, multiple, and multi-layered. Deleuze uses tropes of neuroscience like "neural networks, microbiological interdependency and action potentials" to highlight the materiality of the viewer's body.[12]

Other critics have added further insights into the relevance of embodied perception to film studies. Theorists like Linda Williams, Karin Littau, and Steven Shaviro study the viewer's body as an index of response, while Laura U. Marks, Barbara Kennedy, and Vivian Sobchack concentrate more on the viewer's body actively participating in the cinematic discourse and imparting to the latter a new dimension by generating new meanings through the working of the sensory organs.[13] Such an approach emphasizes how the text of the film and the body of the viewer interact with each other, thereby enriching both the film and its viewer.

"Gooseflesh" and "Tickles": Hitchcock and Corporeality

In many ways, Hitchcock lends himself well to a corporeal approach. His most famous brand is his own body. The sketch of his face is a logo everyone is familiar with; his cameo appearances are cinematic moments that the audience eagerly waits for, and his regular appearances on television made him a household figure. But this habitual drawing of attention to his corporeal self extends far beyond his cameos to a pronounced concern for physicality in his films and insistent attention to bodily responses to his films. His fanciful speculation on a new technology was true to the spirit of what he wanted to accomplish with the cinematic tools he had:

> In the distant future, they will have what I call "the Tickles." People will go into a big darkened auditorium and they will be mass-hypnotized. Instead of identifying themselves with the characters on the screen, they will be that character, and when they buy their ticket, they will be able to choose which character they want to be. They will suffer all of the agonies and enjoy the romance with a beautiful woman or handsome man. I call them "the Tickles," because when a character is tickled, the audience will feel it.[14]

Hitchcock requires his audience to be bodily involved; he demands a visceral engagement where the viewer's senses would be entangled with the very process of watching his films.

The viewer's corporeal engagement was Hitchcock's objective from the very beginning of his filmmaking career. Mardy Grothe reports that

> Passing through French customs early in his career, Alfred Hitchcock was questioned by a suspicious inspector who looked quizzically at the occupation stated on the passport: "Producer." The customs official asked, "What do you produce?" Hitchcock answered: *Gooseflesh*.[15]

It is critical to note that Hitchcock does this by more than sight and sound, as Paul Elliott demonstrates so persuasively in *Hitchcock and the Cinema of Sensation,* which in particular shifts our focus from the conventional emphasis on the centrality of the gaze to a new awareness of the centrality of the body in Hitchcock films. Elliott's close reading of the postmodern scopic regime considers how embodied experience and affective sensations are generated through visuals.[16] By applying the theory of haptic visuality, Elliott brings the corporeality of characters on and off screen right at the center of Hitchcock studies. Elliott's broad approach fully supports and in fact includes attention to the particular element of embodied spectatorship that I focus on here specifically, the sense of smell, which in some respects may seem like an unlikely component of cinematic representation and the spectatorial experience. He chooses *Shadow of a Doubt* (1943) as a film where the "smellscapes" of Santa Rosa and Philadelphia are powerfully and meaningfully evoked. Building on readings by Robin Wood and Donald Spoto of *The Shadow of a Doubt* as a study in duality with their numerous recounting of the motif of the double, Elliott shows how this duality is experienced by the viewers through their olfactory sense as well as their vision.[17] We are provided with an initial contrast and then a gradual intermingling of a large city's filthy smells and the fresh smells of a small town. For example, Uncle Charlie in a dinner table conversation derides the world as a "foul sty" and equates the "lazy" widows of the world to "fat pigs" wallowing in their grimy wealth, bringing forth a perplexing hint of foul smell right in the middle of a sumptuous meal being enjoyed by an otherwise contented family.

Taking a cue from Elliott's analysis of *The Shadow of a Doubt,* I trace *Psycho*'s engagement of the non-visual senses of the viewer, especially their sense of smell, thereby generating meaning within their own body. I explore how, apart from sight and sound, smell is a key component of the entire process of responding to and interpreting *Psycho,* integrated thematically into what the film is about and activating an intersensory and multisensory experience of watching the film.

Figure 1

"Olfaction Gone Bad": Marion and the Smells of a Bathroom

Smell as the principal sensory experience of a film is quite infrequent in Hitchcock's *oeuvre*. While tactile and gustatory experiences abound in the sensual narratives of his films, the olfactory experience must be teased out through minute and careful rummaging. Although smelling is primarily a chemically induced process, it can be embodied in or otherwise associated with memories. As Marks argues, films can communicate smell through identification with an on-screen character involved in the act of sniffing, or through the synaesthetic appeal of on-screen images, for instance, close shots that provoke our touch-smell associations.

Marion Crane (Janet Leigh), the protagonist of the first half of the film, is associated with smell from the very beginning. Marion is first seen as Hitchcock's camera enters a stuffy hotel room through a small opening of a window sash. We see a poorly lit chamber with cheap furniture around. Sam Loomis (John Gavin) is seen wiping his body with a towel and then nestling with Marion on the bed, with a slow table fan buzzing in the background—two lovers meeting secretly during lunch break (fig. 1).

Phoenix at "Two-Forty Three P.M.," as the film specifies, can be quite warm even in December, as Sam confirms: "It's Friday

anyway . . . and hot" (3).[18] The wiping of Sam's body makes
us aware of his sweat, and the snuggling of the lovers
immediately after that associates Marion with a postcoital
whiff as she dresses for her office after the lovemaking. The
exchange that follows becomes gradually uncomfortable as
the two lovers' sense of entrapment in their financial woes
is exposed and adds to the sweaty smell of the small,
cramped room.

As the film progresses, specifically after Marion steals
forty thousand dollars, she is constantly connected with
images that are usually associated with stench: petrol pump,
garage, bathrooms, commode, drain, blood, and finally
swamp. Cramped unventilated spaces like a run-down hotel
room, the interior of a car, and a garage washroom, coupled
with the immoral act of stealing, manipulate our sense of smell
with its long-inherited cultural codes that tie "moral
impropriety" with "stench." Speaking of the cultural hierarchy
of smell, Classen hints at our moral prejudice that informs
such hierarchy:

> It is evident in most such cases that the stench
> ascribed to the other is far less a response to an actual
> perception of the odor of the other than a potent
> metaphor for the social decay it is feared the other,
> often simply by virtue of being "other," will cause in
> the established order. On a small scale, we say that
> something or someone "stinks" when it disagrees
> with our notion of propriety; on a large scale, we
> apply this metaphor to whole groups of people.[19]

Marion's act of stealing "disagrees with our notion of
propriety" and we are culturally prone to labeling her as
someone who "stinks." A woman who has committed the
"sin" of fornication and is a thief dies in a bathroom and we
draw a straight line that connects "foul smell" with "foul
deeds." The bathroom, a place associated with bodily waste,
becomes a "fitting" site for the murder of a "morally corrupt"
and "promiscuous" woman. As William Ian Miller states:

Figure 2

"It is nearly impossible to keep bad smells out of the moral domain. The language of sin and wickedness is the language of olfaction gone bad."[20] Culture's age-old olfactory coding makes for a complacent and convenient explanation that some bodies are more prone to violent deaths (for instance, the victims of Jack the Ripper) in murky, smelly spaces like a dingy dark alley or a shabby unused lot or a motel bathroom on a rough lonely highway night. In *Psycho*, the smell of waste linked to a bathroom thus easily wafts from a stigmatized body of a female thief. For some, the immorality of her act is washed away with the blood and the dirt of her tired body down the gaping drain. The "foul odor" of her act becomes one with the "foul odor" of the space she breathes her last.

The entire bathroom episode is full of olfactory associations. Marion takes a piece of paper, calculates the amount of the stolen money spent, shreds the paper, and then flushes the shreds down the commode (fig. 2). The paper with the calculation of the money stolen is thus symbolic "filth" that is flushed out, reminding us of Tania Modleski's statement that Marion is allied with "filthy lucre" in *Psycho*.[21] Additionally, the shots of blood flowing down Marion's legs after she is stabbed are not shown once as flowing from the wounds of the abdomen. Seen independently, the blood spreading over the bathtub, and trickling down the drain is

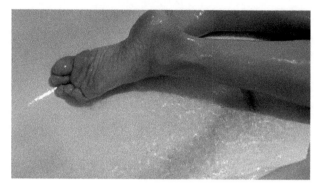

Figure 3

perhaps a visual reminder of menstrual blood with its usual association with "stink" (fig. 3). The close shots of a commode, the mouth of the drain, and blood flowing down Marion's legs taken together is a visual weaving of a disturbing mesh of olfactory connections between filth, depravity, death, desecration, excrement, and effluvium.

While Mrs. Bates reeks of death and decaying skin, Marion provides us with the scatological smells of the living. After Marion's murder, when Norman Bates (Anthony Perkins) enters the bathroom and discovers the dead body of Marion, his first instinct is to cover his mouth (fig. 4).

Until this point in the narrative, the film makes us identify ourselves with Marion. Until the murder of Marion, we are constantly and literally with her. Through eye-line matches, Hitchcock makes us see what Marion sees. Her inner monologues in voiceover make us participate in her world of desperation and fear, and when we are fully enmeshed in her life she is suddenly killed off, leaving us stunned and bewildered. After this abrupt killing of Marion with whom we have begun the journey of this drama, the director now forces us to search for another character through whom we can cling to the narrative. At such a crucial juncture enters Norman, apparently innocent, and like us, shocked at such

Figure 4

brutality. We immediately switch sides and start experiencing the aftermath of the violence through him. Norman's shielding of his mouth after the discovery of Marion's murder may be read as a natural response to the shock of such a brutal scene. But it may also be interpreted as an attempt to prevent a sense of nausea that can overcome a person by the overwhelming sight and stench of blood, reminding us of Kant's words at the beginning of this essay, "filth seems to arouse nausea, not so much through what is repugnant to the eyes and tongue as through the stench that we presume it has." Unlike poisoning or strangling or burning, stabbing means bleeding to death. We share with Norman the disconcerting stench of a stabbed victim.

Norman's first word to describe Cabin No. 1 is "stuffy." He opens the window immediately after entering the room with Marion, letting in fresh air. Later, after discovering the corpse of Marion, he first shuts the window and the door, making the room "stuffy" again. The cabin has no ventilation when Norman wipes off Marion's blood. Thus, the smell of blood cannot escape the room. Successive close shots of blood on the bathroom floor, on Norman's hands, in the wash basin, and in the bathtub (figs. 5, 6, and 7) draw us into olfactory perception. The overwhelming visual plenitude of blood opens up viewers' memories and draw out their remembered smell associated with it.

Figure 5

Figure 6

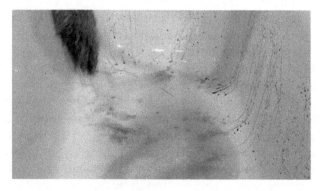

Figure 7

Figure 8

Finally, when we see the car getting sucked into the bog, we are as equally mired in the stink of the swamp as Norman is (fig. 8). The point of identification is so acute that we wait as breathlessly as Norman for the car to sink into the cesspool. The entire process, from cleaning the toilet to disposing of the dead body, is pervaded by a sense of foul play and foul smell. Hitchcock drags us through the entire process of destruction and desecration not only through vision but also through our olfactory senses. Identifying with Norman, we wish fervently for the car to sink so that the evidence of the body may be destroyed and this nightmarish journey, from the unbearable smell-scape of the bathroom to the reeking swamp, may end.

Rotting Flesh and Pickled Skin

While Marion is associated with smells most foul, Mrs. Bates, a preserved corpse, is associated with the smell of the past. Taxidermy is used as a major trope in the film.[22] Apart from the visual fascination that the art offers us, it alerts our olfactory senses as well. Taxidermy, dealing with dead preserved skin, apart from fascinating or repelling a viewer with the thought of blood and guts, also affects our sense of smell. An art that rests on the process of preservation with materials that are themselves perishable, it also brings forth another irony. A taxidermized exhibit is supposed to replace death with the life-like; it is supposed to sanitize and deodorize the metallic smell of a loose carcass and the stench of a decaying specimen with preservatives and chemicals. But the dead skin arranged in the form of a live body and the smell often of glue, sawdust, and preservatives (at times) underlines the smell of death thus veiled. Herein lies a grim irony. The skin once lived can be touched. But its "live-ness" can never be smelt. In the process of remaking a body, the odor of death is never allowed to set in. It is replaced by the odors of additives. A taxidermized body consequently carries the musty smell of preservation, ironically adding to the very deadness of the preserved. In this painstaking effort at capturing life, the smell of a live body somehow eludes us.

Although the smell of blood, the smell of old Mrs. Bates, and the smell of stuffed birds in the motel do not reach us physically, our "synaesthetic memory" (our memory of the stickiness and stench of blood, our memory of putrid flesh, or our memory of smell that comes out of an eviscerated body at the raw meat shop or of roadkill) serves as an experiential reference point that evokes the smell of arrested decay. The preserved birds in Norman's motel in the parlor carry with them not only the visual specter of death but also remind us of all the revolting stink of blood, guts, and preservatives. The birds we see in the motel parlor are predominantly birds of prey that seem very menacing (fig. 9).

In real life, predatory birds are often seen feeding on flesh, particularly rotting flesh. Close shots of these predatory birds dominate the scenes in the Bates parlor. These close encounters with the exhibits, apart from bringing forth the irony of the hunter-hunted binary, also highlight the possibility of "visual sniffing" of those birds and the smells associated with them. When we see them, we also smell them—not only their own bodies, but also the innards of rodents and other smaller creatures that they feed on. The apprehension generated by that smell is carried out literally in the scenes that follow shortly—the brutal stabbings of Marion and Milton Arbogast (Martin Balsam)—where we witness blood and violent death.

Figure 9

"Some Musty Presence": Mrs. Bates's Room

The house where Mrs. Bates is kept is a storehouse of "unrecordable memories of the senses," to use Marks's term.[23] It is a room where opposites, including sensory ones, reside. The stench of old age is juxtaposed with clean sheets, well-pressed clothes, and polished surfaces. Throughout *Psycho*, Mrs. Bates comes across to us as a voice. We do not see her until the end. We are thus left with only one alternative—to generate her materially and situate her in our cinematic experience with the help of any sensory device at our disposal. The director has provided us with a voice and with a setting where she is framed. So, the towering house where she resides needs to be ransacked for clues of her presence. In her ethnographic survey of the relationship between domestic space, interior design, and self-identity, *Home Truths: Gender, Domestic Objects, and Everyday Life,* Sarah Pink attempts an embodied reading of the space within a house where our olfactory, auditory, and tactile senses play a significant part in reading the kind of lives that are lived and shaped there. She explains, "olfactory strategies constituted engagement with other agencies of the home, for example, dust, dog hair and odour, cooking odours, the mustiness of curtains and the 'smell' the house has after going away and leaving it closed up."[24] The interior has a narrative that

Figure 10

interweaves "the visual ('when you look'), olfactory ('to smell fresh') and emotional ('satisfaction')."

As we step inside Mrs. Bates's room with Lila Crane (Vera Miles), apart from the visual clues, our sense of smell helps us fathom the kind of person who may have occupied this space. The whole setting is an amalgamation of past and present brought forth by our olfactory senses. The script reads: "And there is in the room an unmistakably live quality as if even though it is presently unoccupied, it has not been long vacated by some *musty presence*" (120). The smell of "musty presence" that the script speaks of is juxtaposed with smells of soap beside a washbasin and cosmetics and perfumes and fresh powders on the dresser (fig. 10); the dank smell of the traces of a supposedly ill body on the bed is contrasted with the smell of fresh, spotless, well-ironed clothes in the large wardrobe.

The script reads: "[Lila] sees the high wardrobe out of the corner of her eyes, goes to it, hesitantly. She opens one door. Fresh, clean, well pressed dresses hang neatly. Lila opens the other door. The sweaters and dresses and robes hang freely, none in moth-proof, storage-type bags. There is even a well-brushed collar of foxes. Along the floor of the wardrobe is a line of clean, polished shoes" (120). Just as the body of Mrs. Bates is an amalgamation of many opposites (living/dead, active/passive, observer/observed, mother/son), her room

Figure 11

is also characterized by similar contrasts; as death co-exists with life in Mrs. Bates's body, so does the smell of mustiness cohabit with the smell of fresh clothes and toiletries in her room.

The architectural costumery and layout provoke us to respond to Mrs. Bates with non-visual senses. In the absence of her physical presence, we may take recourse to our sense of smell while creating a visual image of her body. Mrs. Bates smells of old age. What we gather from her silhouettes are faint traces of her loose robes, her harsh voice, her disheveled hair, and her sickness. These visual hints also carry with them the clue of mustiness. The mansion in which she is confined and her bedroom that Lila invades are filled with this "musty presence" despite the polished oaks and ornate trinkets. The imagined body of Mrs. Bates seeps into us through what Marks calls the "silent registers" of our sense of smell.[25] We construct Mrs. Bates through the smells of her clothes in the wardrobe, and the unkempt bed which still carries marks of her preserved corpse (fig. 11).

The architecture of the room and the space within it that reflect the typical material culture of Victorian domesticity help the viewers in recreating this "old hag" in their imagination. With Lila we are almost sucked into an ornately textured room—venetian blinds, thick carpet, velvet-covered upholstery, a wide-ranging array of heavy Victorian furnishing, the wardrobe, the crossed bronze hands, the statues, the huge, gilded mirrors, and the bed dominating the entire room with Mother's imprint. The overabundance of objects overwhelms vision and trickles into other senses. The mark of Mother on the bed and the heavy Victorian décor signify a world that has been left behind. The search for Mrs. Bates and her imprint on the bed apprehending her recent occupation of the room make the viewer acutely reliant on sound, smell, and touch experiences. Vision becomes a kind of contact point through which these senses become alert, leading to an embodied perception. This is how Hitchcock presents Stefano's idea of a "musty" presence in Mother's room.

One particularly memorable comment that Mrs. Bates makes about herself suggests her mental condition while evoking her smell. While she is refusing to go to the fruit cellar, she raves, "No! I will not hide in the fruit cellar! . . . Think I'm fruity, huh?" (100). The cellar that is supposed to smell of fresh fruits smells of putrefaction as it contains the remains of a dead and decayed body. The amalgamation reaches a visual climax in the fruit cellar where the parched skin of the dead is dressed in fresh well-pressed clothes. The smell of old age gives way to the stench of decay intermingled with clean-smelling robes.

The constricted spaces of Mrs. Bates's room, the basement and the parlor crammed with preserved birds, evoke forlornness—peopled as they are with bodies bereft of life and the odors of life. These preserved bodies either smell of sawdust and preservatives or they do not smell at all. Every live body has a smell of its own, "good" or "bad." An odorless body is neither alive nor dead.

Norman's Nursery: "Descent Into Disintegration"

Norman Bates is another example of a blend of opposites, including opposite smells. Norman's room, like his mother's, carries the unmistakable stench of time held in confinement. His room, with its tattered toys, cramped tiny bed, Beethoven's *Eroica*, gramophone, and hard-bound nameless

Figure 12

books, is like a nursery where the space along with the boy inhabiting it remains suspended in times past. The unkempt bed with faint traces of Norman's body is an uneasy reminder of Mrs. Bates's (fig. 12). Unmade beds signify neglect and can carry the stench of staleness. We do not find even a small window in the room from where the stale smell can escape. It is as if nothing, not even fresh air, is allowed to enter the room lest it vitiate Norman's museum of his childhood. The layout and interior of the Bates house can be described as, in Chris Baldick's words, a Gothic space:

> For the Gothic effect to be attained, a tale should combine a fearful sense of inheritance in time with a claustrophobic sense of enclosure in space, these two dimensions reinforcing one another to produce an impression of sickening descent into disintegration.[26]

It is through this suffocating internment in claustrophobic spaces that we experience, along with the characters on-screen, the "sickening descent into disintegration."

"Claustrophobic . . . enclosure" and "sickening descent into disintegration" have heavy olfactory connotations. In *The Foul and the Fragrant*, Alain Corbin speaks of putrefaction theory of the eighteenth century, which hypothesized that "walls . . . preserved odors."[27] Norman's room is a halted room of a child, a confined narrow space with no hint of movement. The walls, the toys, the bed and other accessories preserve "odors" of the past—odors that are not allowed to escape. It is this putrid sense of everything arrested that greets Lila in the Bates House. Like the stuffed birds on the motel wall and the preserved mother in the basement, the rooms have also been kept static, neither abandoned nor renovated. Everything in the Bates world remains still and confined. With confinement comes the rancid stench of decay and disease.

The Dank Dystopia of Psycho

For French film scholars of the 1960s and 1970s, Hitchcock is a great modernist thinker and a great manipulator of form. While Claude Chabrol and Eric Rohmer see him as a philosopher of the "Kantian" mode, Jean Douchet argues that it is the "intellectual world" of the Hitchcockian *oeuvre* that enables his viewers to transcend the baser aspects of the body.[28] While recognizing the importance of terror in Hitchcock films, however, Douchet also argues that terror is "not the ultimate goal pursued by Hitchcock." He assigns a "mission" to Hitchcock's "suspense": "And this mission is cathartic. The spectator has to 'undo his repressions' in a psychoanalytical sense, confess himself on a logical plane, purify himself on a spiritual level" (17). Speaking of *Rear Window*, Douchet labels feelings of desire and fear that are aroused by Hitchcock as "low" and "vile": "Hitchcock first excites vile and low feelings in his public" (18) that can only be transcended later with the aid of the intellectual world, "devoid of any passion, detached from subjectivity, freed of all unhealthy curiosity" (22). In sharp contrast to this reading is Hitchcock's warning in one of the reissued posters of *Rear Window* where he holds a placard that reads: "I have no objection if you see 'Rear Window' twenty times. This motion picture has enough merit to stand up under any number of viewings. But please do not anticipate those *deliciously terrifying* scenes that *make you scream. Hold your breath* until the scenes actually appear on the screen. *Then let go.*" The warning continues: "See it! — *If your nerves can stand it* after Psycho!" (emphasis added).[29]

The objective perhaps is not entirely to transcend the "low" and "vile" feelings, or to "purify" oneself or free oneself from "unhealthy curiosity," as argued by Douchet. Hitchcock's films may instead make us realize that there is no escape from such "low" and "vile" emotions, nor can one free oneself from the "unhealthy curiosity" that his films and its intriguing characters evoke. We feel "cabined" and "cribbed" in these suffocating spaces where random violence is a given.

The violent shower murder set-piece coupled with a constant presence of enclosed claustrophobic spaces in *Psycho* — from the dark and sparse hotel room in Phoenix to the stifling office where Marion works, to stuffy cars, to dirty garages and bathrooms, to the airless motel parlor, to the ever-forbidding Bates house, to the fruit cellar, and finally to a stark prison cell — jar our senses. *Psycho's* settings and the smells they conjure bring home to the viewer the pathos and the fear of what Norman says:

> You know what I think? I think we're all in our private traps, clamped in them, and none of us can ever climb out. We scratch and claw . . . but only at the air, only at each other, and for all of it, we never budge an inch. (45-46)

It is through this sense of confinement coupled with words like "dampness" and "dank" used by Norman that we get a strong sharp whiff of the Bates world. Norman, while interacting with Arbogast, informs him that he abhors the smell of "dampness": "Today's linen day. I change all the beds once a week, whether they've been used or not . . . *dampness*. I hate the smell of *dampness* . . . It's such a *dank* smell" (71, emphasis added). The word "dank" resurfaces when Mrs. Bates protests vehemently against being confined in the fruit cellar: "In that *dank* fruit cellar? No! You hid me there once, boy, and you won't do it again! Not ever again!" (101, emphasis added).

The words "dank" and "dampness" are used for the smell that pervades the entire film. The film opens with the skyscape

of Phoenix, Arizona, and quickly progresses to the downtown.
The opening scene has three establishing shots as the camera
pans over the city. Three dissolves cover the city from left to
right in a slow steady pace. Although it is difficult to
distinguish a major change of scene, we can discern a slight
alteration in the layout and the tenor of the shots as one
dissolve follows the other. We can see fewer cars, an empty car
lot, and the buildings as older and shabbier. The dimness
becomes more pronounced, the shadows longer, as the camera
focuses on a window with hints of a dark interior. As the script
reads, "It is darker and shabby with age and industry. We see
railroad tracks, smokestacks, wholesale fruit and vegetable
markets, old municipal buildings, empty lots" (1).
Interestingly, the script pinpoints "smokestacks" and "fruit
and vegetable markets" that evoke olfactory associations.
Stefano uses the smell of smokestacks and wholesale food
markets to evoke a sense of the old and the familiar here.
Although the camera is too far away for the viewers to detect
these settings, Hitchcock's camera takes those olfactory hints
into the private space of a tawdry hotel room with its stale
sandwich kept untouched on a well-worn table.

Not once do we feel the presence of a soothing smell in
Psycho. The experience is anything but cathartic. The
reactions of bodies within and beyond the screen
reinforce a tale of hapless mortals trapped in a world that
smells of mustiness and preservatives. While Mrs. Bates
is forced to remain confined either in her room or in the
basement, Marion's alternatives remain either a small
downtown hotel room or Sam's small room at the back of a
hardware store. Marion's attempt to come out of that trap,
like the attempts of Mrs. Bates, is unsuccessful. She says, "I
stepped into a private trap back there [Phoenix]—and I want
to go back and try to pull myself out before it's too late for
me, too," not knowing that it is already too late for her (49).
It is also too late for Norman, a young man who cleans sheets
once every week to avoid the smell of dankness, but
ironically dons the material accessories of an old woman to
become a body that smells of old age.

Notes

I am deeply indebted to Sidney Gottlieb for his thorough comments and insightful observations that have improved my paper immensely.

1. William Shakespeare, *Macbeth*, ed. Kenneth Muir (New York: Methuen, 1984).

2. For example, see Alain Corbin, *The Foul and the Fragrant: Odor and the Social Imagination* (Oxford: Berg Publishers, 2000); Constance Classen, "The Odor of the Other: Olfactory Symbolism and Cultural Categories," *Ethos* 20, no. 2 (1992): 133-66; and William Ian Miller, *The Anatomy of Disgust* (Cambridge: Harvard University Press, 1997).

3. Constance Classen, David Howes, and Anthony Synnott, *Aroma: The Cultural History of Smell* (New York: Routledge, 1994), 3.

4. Immanuel Kant, *Anthropology from a Pragmatic Point of View* (1798), trans. and ed. Robert B. Louden (Cambridge: Cambridge University Press, 2006), 50.

5. Sigmund Freud, *Civilization and its Discontents* (1930), trans. James Strachey (New York: W.W. Norton, 2010), 78-79.

6. Maurice Merleau-Ponty, *Phenomenology of Perception*, trans. Colin Smith (New York: Routledge and Kegan Paul, 1962), xvi-xvii.

7. David MacDougall, *The Corporeal Image: Film, Ethnography, and the Senses* (Princeton: Princeton University Press, 2006), 20.

8. MacDougall, *The Corporeal Image*, 20, 25.

9. Vivian Sobchack, "What My Fingers Knew: The Cinesthetic Subject, or Vision in the Flesh," in *Carnal Thoughts: Embodiment and Moving Image Culture* (Berkeley and Los Angeles: University of California Press, 2004), 53-84.

10. Walter Benjamin, "The Work of Art in the Age of Mechanical Reproduction" (1935), trans. J.A. Underwood (Penguin Random House, 2008), ebook, 1-38.

11. Siegfried Kracauer, *Theory of Film: The Redemption of Physical Reality* (Princeton: Princeton University Press, 1960), xxi.

12. Quoted in Paul Elliott, *Hitchcock and the Cinema of Sensations: Embodied Film Theory and Cinematic Reception* (New York: I.B. Tauris, 2011), Kindle edition, Loc.700.

13. See, for example, Linda Williams, "Film Bodies: Gender, Genre, and Excess," *Film Quarterly* 44, no. 4 (1991); Karin

Littau, *Theories of Reading: Books, Bodies, and Bibliomania* (Malden, MA: Polity Press, 2006), especially "The Role of Affect in Literary Criticism" (83-102) and "The Reader in Theory" (103-24); Steven Shaviro, *The Cinematic Body* (Minneapolis: University of Minnesota Press, 1993); Laura U. Marks, *The Skin of the Film: Intercultural Cinema, Embodiment, and the Senses* (Durham: Duke University Press, 2000); Barbara M. Kennedy, *Deleuze and Cinema: The Aesthetics of Sensation* (Edinburgh: Edinbugh University Press, 2002); and Vivian Sobchak, *Carnal Thoughts*.

14. Quoted in Charlotte Chandler, *It's Only a Movie: Alfred Hitchcock: A Personal Biography* (New York: Simon and Schuster, 2005), 40.

15. Mardy Grothe, *Viva la Repartee* (New York: HarperCollins, 2005), 57.

16. Elliott, *Hitchcock and the Cinema of Sensations,* Loc. 902.

17. Robin Wood, *Hitchcock's Films Revisited* (New York: Columbia University Press, 2002), 297-98; Donald Spoto, *The Dark Side of Genius: The Life of Alfred Hitchcock* (New York: Da Capo Press, 1999), 262-65.

18. Joseph Stefano, *Psycho*, 11/10/59 script, online at https://assets.scriptslug.com/live/pdf/scripts/psycho-1960.pdf. All quotations from the script are cited by page number in the text of my essay.

19. Classen, "The Odor of the Other," 135.

20. Miller, *The Anatomy of Disgust*, 77-78.

21. Tania Modleski, *The Women Who Knew Too Much: Hitchcock and Feminist Theory* (New York: Routledge, 2005), 109.

22. See Subarna Mondal, *Alfred Hitchcock's* Psycho *and Taxidermy: Fashioning Corpses* (New York: Bloomsbury Academic, 2024).

23. Marks, *The Skin of the Film*, 5.

24. Sarah Pink, *Home Truths: Gender, Domestic Objects, and Everyday Life* (Oxford: Berg Publishers, 2004), 2.

25. Marks, *The Skin of the Film*, 5.

26. Chris Baldick, ed. *The Oxford Book of Gothic Tales* (New York: Oxford University Press, 2001), xix.

27. Corbin, *The Foul and the Fragrant*, 26.

28. Eric Rohmer and Claude Chabrol, *Hitchcock: The First Forty-Four Films*, trans. Stanley Hochman (New York: Frederick Ungar Publishing Co., 1979), 124; Jean Douchet, "Hitch and His Public," trans. Verena Andermatt Conley, in *A Hitchcock Reader*, ed. Marshall

Deutelbaum and Leland Poague (Ames: Iowa State University Press, 2009), 10. Further references to Douchet will be cited by page number in the text of my essay.

29. See this image online at https://www.allposters.com/-sp/Rear-Window-Alfred-Hitchcock-James-Stewart-Grace-Kelly-1954-Posters_i15561531_.htm?UPI=Q1BUBS30&PODConfigID=9201946&sOrigID=16889.

ELISABETH KARLIN

Lamb to the Slaughter

Laurence Leamer, *Hitchcock's Blondes: The Unforgettable Women Behind the Legendary Director's Dark Obsession*. New York: G.P. Putnam's Sons, 2023. 336 pp. $29.00 cloth.

In interviews, Alfred Hitchcock often fondly remembered how his father called him his "little lamb without a spot." And that was pretty much how the public saw the fellow with the deadpan avuncularity and puckish presence. He was someone who may have talked a good game of murder but who wouldn't hurt a fly. Then, he died and hot on death's heels, Donald Spoto's biography, *The Dark Side of Genius* (1983) came barreling breathlessly into view.[1] With it Spoto brought forth seamy speculations about the director's personal life and inner thoughts, going so far as to charge him with the merciless torment of Tippi Hedren. And that is how the little lamb got his spots.

Once he was spotted by Spoto, the perception at large of Hitchcock shifted but did not entirely hold. Many readers found the book to be a comprehensive enough biography of the genius but a scabrous and not entirely convincing case of his dark side. At that, Spoto dug in his heels and published *Spellbound by Beauty: Alfred Hitchcock and His Leading Ladies* (2008), where in excruciating detail, reaching hyperbole, he wallowed in the muck and mire—largely imagined—of practically every relationship Hitchcock ever had with an actress.[2] Finally, for his *coup de grâce*, Spoto ushered in *The Girl* (2012), an HBO film based on Tippi Hedren's ever-varying and escalating recollections, and for which he was creative consultant.[3] Known as "the Hitchcock sexual harassment flick," it was widely promoted and arrived before #MeToo was coined but lingered in the collective consciousness long enough for that movement's explosion. The single charge, leveled by Hedren, morphed into widespread assumptions and a rush to judgement that lumped Hitchcock in with some vile company. Now when his name came up in popular discourse, words like "creepy" and "pervy" came attached to it, the more charitable allowing that he was a creepy and pervy genius.

What does it mean to defend Alfred Hitchcock? In the face of a promulgating impression that he was a pathological misogynist, does one deny he was such a brute? To do so, one could cite the uncertain evidence against him, along with the affectionate reminiscences of the vast majority of the women he worked with. Or does one prefer to comprehend his attitudes toward women through his films? What he gave us in those films were women of thought, action, and vision—an unusual look for leading ladies at the time. These women are active characters but beyond that, in the course of their stories they are allowed a moral arc in which they can develop conscientious world views—retaining their lively irreverence while unearthing their grit and generous spirits. As I've said before—a Hitchcock woman is never just a wife, just a girlfriend, just a mother, and certainly, never just a blonde.[4]

Weary of playing defense, it's only natural that I would approach Lawrence Leamer's new book, *Hitchcock's Blondes*, a volume that arrives with the subtitle "The unforgettable women behind the legendary director's dark obsession," with interest but also heaving a Vandamm-like sigh of "Blondes? Must we?" Even before getting to the dark roots of blonde obsession that Leamer promises, one might reconsider the tired trope of the Hitchcock Blonde. Classifying the heroines of Hitchcock to a singular vision of an icy, mysterious blonde is not only reductive: it is false. While Hitchcock himself may have promoted the idea of the "Hitchcock blonde," it continues to mislead us when discussing the women in his films. Some are blonde, some are not. The only figure who realizes everyone's idea of the unattainable Hitchcock blonde is the spectral Madeleine Elster. But Madeleine is not real, merely a disguise worn by her exact opposite, a dark-haired, very available, and impressively canny, shopgirl. Even among the blondes, none of them conforms to this imaginary breed that has rooted itself in popular culture with the the help of critics, scholars, and Hitchcock himself. How many worlds apart is Francie Stevens, who dines at the best Riviera hotels, from Marion Crane and her sad sandwich at a Phoenix fleabag? How different are the days of Dr. Constance Peterson from the nights of playgirl Melanie Daniels? The lot of them vary wildly from social and economic status to temperament. If we insist on sorting the Hitchcock blonde as a species, we have to understand that this is a strain that cannot be simply defined.

Leamer, a prolific chronicler of celebrities, looks at eight actresses who, in his view, elucidate the best work and the worst character traits of Hitchcock. He comes to this subject fresh off the success of *Capote's Women*, in which he showcased the socialites known as Capote's "swans" and is the source material for the recent television series *Feud: Capote vs. The Swans* (2024).[5] In *Hitchcock's Blondes*, he believes he has struck on a whole new bevy. But are the Hitchcock women really swans? You could say Grace Kelly filled that designation: after all, she did play the eponymous royal bird in the film of Molnar's play (*The Swan* [1956], directed by Charles Vidor). Tippi Hedren made an attempt at swanhood but she lacked Kelly's composed glide, which I guess tags her as a "swannabe." In the world of waterfowl, though, I prefer to see the Hitchcock heroines as a flock of lovely ducks. There is, after all, only one genus of swans, whereas ducks are diversified.

Hitchcock's Blondes covers much of the same trampled ground as *Spellbound by Beauty* but with a more benign approach and a welcome surprise twist at the end. Leamer doesn't have Spoto's long Hitchcock history—a bizarre journey that took him from acolyte to assassin. Spoto's first book, *The Art of Alfred Hitchcock*, published in 1976, was a passionate and insightful overview of all the films that sent many (I among them) on their way to fully fledged Hitchcock adherence. It began with a foreword by Grace Kelly that read "This book is about someone I love and respect . . . I [also] came to know him as a warm and understanding human being."[6] That Spoto should later write what he called "The story of a man so unhappy, so full of self-loathing, so lonely and friendless that his satisfactions came as much from asserting power as from spinning fantasies and acquiring wealth" was a jolt.[7]

In contrast to Spoto, Leamer presents the more detached view of a writer on assignment. Dabbling in the world of Hitchcock, he has done the research and can give workmanlike retellings of plot and analysis suitable for those with a glancing knowledge and interest in film. Still, in profiling the eight women, he attempts to build a premise that in spite of their memorable work with Hitchcock, it may have been done at a cost to their well-being. He tells us: "As these actresses made memorable films with Hitchcock he projected his complicated, tortured attitude toward women on the screen."[8]

Leamer's strength is gathering gossip, and while that may satisfy our natural nosiness, he has a tendency to draw some far-fetched inferences from his scuttlebutt. For example, he interprets a case of wine sent to Gregory Peck as "Hitchcock attempting to show his superiority over this actor who possessed the woman [Ingrid Bergman] he wanted for himself" (65). The reckless stretching and hypothesizing includes this gratuitous diagnosis from a Dr. Heath King, a psychoanalyst who taught a course on American film at Yale, but as far as we knowdid not ever have Mr. Hitchcock in his consulting room:

It is clear to me Hitchcock had Asperger's syndrome, now included in autism spectrum disorder. He was a loner, an ogler, who sublimated his lack of sex into a voyeuristic cinema technique. The anxiety and fear he evoked in his films were a projection of his own inner anxiety and fear of an actual personal encounter where he was not in control . . . This lack of empathy was integral to Hitchcock's enormous gifts. (9)

How little resemblance this portrayal bears to the cosmopolitan *bon vivant* who held court weekly at Chasen's when not entertaining friends and colleagues at home! If having inner fears and anxieties puts one on the autism scale, then I'd say we're all on that spectrum. Our own fears and anxieties are exactly why his pictures work on us so viscerally. As to a lack of empathy, I can't pretend to understand how that would be integral to anyone's artistic gifts or how such sociopathy would apply to Hitchcock.

In advancing his theory that Hitchcock must have enjoyed seeing women suffer (and all the better if she's a blonde), Leamer, like Spoto, rests his conclusions on what he evidently sees as some mysterious access to the hidden workings of Hitchcock's head:

Creating a Pygmalion appears a glorious thing when it is Professor Henry Higgins transforming the street waif Eliza Doolittle into a beauty who can masquerade as a princess in *My Fair Lady*. But when that journey is about sexual power—a gentleman not lusting after his ideal in his book-lined study, but actually creating her in the flesh—the dark side of such a pursuit is revealed. And Hitchcock did it again and again in his films, getting off on it every time. And his audiences got off on it too. . . . Hitchcock took what in real life would likely have been considered a sick fixation on the icy, unattainable blond woman and turned it into a central part of his artistic dream. In time, Hitchcock's fantasies about the actresses who starred in his films consumed much of his creative energy—and ultimately defined a large part of his legacy. (8)[9]

Leamer hopscotches over some of the most considerable leading ladies in Hitchcock, understandably excluding the many non-blondes and others perhaps not blonde enough. But he curiously omits two mega-stars who couldn't be blonder. Carole Lombard is certainly the apotheosis of the elegant blonde Leamer is fixed on, but her breezy and loving friendship with Hitchcock apparently doesn't fit into the narrative. Nor does Doris Day, who came to do a job and did it (and how!). Day's only concern was that it was hard to tell if she was pleasing him. She was.

In his litany of transgressions, Leamer suggests that Hitchcock came close to killing June Tripp in *The Lodger* by having her repeat a scene of running upstairs with a ruptured appendix, though there is no indication that he knew of her condition. Leamer follows that with the discomfort Madeleine Carroll had to endure by being handcuffed to Robert Donat for long hours while making *The 39 Steps* (1935). Add to that the ordeal Tippi Hedren went through for the attic scene in *The Birds* (1963). There is no doubt these were difficult situations to perform in, and they illustrate that in striving to achieve the effects he was after, Hitchcock could be insensitive to the limits of actors (he wouldn't be the first director there), but it is not evidence of sadistic joy.

Sometimes in sorting through Hitchcock's "ugly and demeaning" offenses (11), Leamer mixes up the real with the fictional. One might think from this book that he actually had Eva Marie Saint hanging on to Mount Rushmore for dear life while making *North by Northwest* (1959) or that Janet Leigh somehow lived to tell about being stabbed in the shower in *Psycho* (1960). Supposed instances of abuse fade in their shock value as the book wears on: Ingrid Bergman and Grace Kelly endured being admired as Hitchcock's ideal women and managed to carry on despite his possible infatuation with them, though he never did anything about those feelings and they had no deleterious effects on those long and lasting friendships. Kim Novak was forced to wear a gray suit and black shoes in *Vertigo* (1958). Imagine!

Enter Tippi Hedren, with the one serious rap against the man. It's a grievance that remains unclear, shrouded in a vague and variable accusation that has snowballed through the years. At one time she called him a fabulous director who taught her everything about acting. Later, she insisted he did nothing but micromanage her performance and ruin her career. In the 1970s there was a round table interview of Hitchcock leading ladies. It's a jolly gabfest with Suzanne Pleshette, Janet Leigh, Eva Marie Saint, Karen Black, and yes, Tippi too. And while Hedren does come off as the least collegial and most self-conscious of the bunch, she says nothing to indicate that she doesn't share in the group's affection for Hitchcock. Asked by the moderator about having called Hitchcock "fat" to his face (she actually called him a "fat pig," according to witnesses), Hedren responds: "I may have done that. I don't remember. That could have happened. I don't remember that."[10]

Hedren once said "He was almost obsessed with me. And it's very difficult to be the object of someone's obsession. I never talked about it for twenty years because I didn't want to think about it in the wrong light. I felt such empathy for Hitch, to have such strong feelings and not have them returned is very difficult."[11] But with passing time and Spoto by her side taking notes, that compassionate and touching assessment of their troubled partnership mutated years after into her characterization of Hitchcock as "evil and deviant to the point of dangerous."[12]

It is in Hedren's story that Leamer ventures off the well-worn track to offer a much different perspective on the imbroglio, though in doing so, he derails the premise of his book. Where Spoto ingratiated himself with Hedren and inserted himself into her life, Leamer's far less fawning view of the actress enables him to come to an unexpected clear-eyed assessment. He collects witness accounts from those who were on hand during the shooting of *Marnie*, including Hedren's stepson and screenwriter Jay Presson Allen. Even Bernard Herrmann weighs in, noting that Hedren was "both untalented and exploitative of Hitchcock's obvious infatuation" (262). The ever-ready expert witness Dr. King is back to label Hedren as a "Calculating narcissist . . . . It was perfectly in line with her to wait until Hitchcock died to attack him" (270). Leamer is cautious about throwing his own darts at Hedren and comes up with a fair analysis:

> It may have happened just as Hedren said it did, but it is also possible the actress misread this. Hedren had the most literal of minds. Certain subtleties and nuances sailed beyond her. Hitchcock had a wicked sense of humor. He sometimes said things he did not mean and would have been startled to see them acted upon. (253)

Leamer, who up to this point in the book has himself assigned dark and malevolent intentions to Hitchcock's quips and innuendos, contradicts his own narrative here but his untangling of the twisted strands of Hedren and Hitchcock is sensible and includes an account of her post-Hitchcock career that exonerates him from ongoing malice, noting that "The director held her contract, but he never once used her again. Beyond that, there is no evidence he set out to ruin her or did anything but move on" (265).

Her life did go on, and she found what may have been her true calling in her work with lions and the creation of her Shambala Preserve (rewarding Donald Spoto with a position on its board). In husband Noel Marshall, she had a much more controlling partner than Hitchcock ever was, and in Leamer's compelling report of the making of their film *Roar* (1981), he plainly indicts Hedren for subjecting her own daughter to far more danger than Hitchcock ever did to any actor. He tells us that "During the filming [of *Roar*] the big cats wounded at least seventy cast and crew members" (269).

There is no question that bits of Hitchcock's behavior would be unacceptable now. His delight in using pranks and suggestive remarks to get a rise out of people—especially women—might not be tolerated today. What may have been regarded as impish then would be deemed offensive now.

And if he did make any kind of sexual proposition to Tippi Hedren (something she was never forthright about), it should not be minimized as mere mischief. But we have to be careful how we apply twenty-first-century expectations and standards to twentieth-century individuals.

The craft of acting doesn't interest Leamer much (to be fair, it didn't interest Hitchcock either), so we don't learn a lot about these actresses as professionals, but we do get a lot of information about their relations with men. He spends a lot of ink on Grace Kelly's sexual shrewdness and makes the mystifying assertion that "In Hitchcock's scenario man was always the aggressor and the woman his conquest. He could hardly imagine a woman manipulating a man into bed, but that's how it often was with Grace" (97). What? Has he met Alicia Huberman or Eve Kendall or Francie Stevens, or any of the army of sexually confident women of Hitchcock? This odd representation of "Hitchcock's scenario" ostensibly fashioned to suit his narrative is so faulty that it throws into doubt Leamer's precision in reading Hitchcock's work.

One thing that *Hitchcock's Blondes* makes inadvertently clear is that the most dramatic turns in the lives of these women, the suffering and troubles that they faced, had nothing to do with Hitchcock: Kim Novak's mental illness, inherited from her father and exacerbated by childhood trauma; Grace Kelly's overbearing parents; the excoriation of Ingrid Bergman in the press and U.S. Congress; the suicide of Janet Leigh's parasitic father. Instead, it looks like the time they spent on a Hitchcock set was a welcome relief from the more destructive forces in their lives. And though Hitchcock may have felt abandoned by his two favorite leading ladies, he had no role in their defection. One can imagine how difficult it must have been for him to lose both to European royalty—Bergman to Roberto Rossellini, the king of Italian neorealism, and Kelly to an actual prince. Here, Leamer conveys an apt sense of sorrow in the regrettable tale of how Kelly's family goaded her into the marriage that signaled the death of Grace Kelly the actress and the birth of Her Serene Highness.

Some soft and incidental sexism runs through *Hitchcock's Blondes* that is reflective of the author but not his subject. The pesky possessiveness of the title suggests that these women were hatched by Hitchcock and in effect, it objectifies them. The cataloging of their scores of affairs are littered throughout with phrases like "Adolphson still wanted a bite out of that sweet apple" (52)—the apple being Ingrid Bergman; or "Milland was not beyond sampling the sweets that passed his way" (109)—the sweets being women; or "When a delicious dish is set before a man of Rossellini's appetites, he must partake, and Bergman was a succulent main course" (81). And when he points out that Hitchcock did not have sex with any actress, he adds "That did not mean Hitchcock was disinterested in sex. He was obsessed with it. Like a street urchin standing at the window of a candy store, his nose pressed against the plate glass, he could not taste any of the sweet delights that lay within" (9). These allusions to females as food could make a modern woman wince. Also, he seems to equate normalcy for a woman with a happy marriage and children:

> Some actresses reach a point in their lives where their maternal instincts overwhelm their professional drives, and they choose motherhood over the claims of stardom. (139)

This is a conclusion full of male presumption, and he reinforces it with this oblique tribute to Eva Marie Saint:

> [Her] most significant achievement—one for which there is no award—is to have maintained a long, honorable career as an actress while not sacrificing her husband, children, and family for a moment. (197)

Would anyone ever suggest that putting family first was a man's most significant achievement? Of the screenwriter Jay Presson Allen, he writes: "To get her way, she used a full measure of female guile" (261). This kind of unconscious gender bias makes one wonder if this particular man, no matter how well-intentioned, should be making judgments on how another man views women.

The most significant woman in Hitchcock's life was of course his wife Alma Reville, about whom Leamer claims: "Hitchcock considered Alma, like most women, a lesser being. And she, in some measure accepted that appellation" (27). A lesser being who began as a mentor and became his professional partner and the one person who he commonly deferred to? Hitchcock was among the most faithful and uxorious of husbands. Yet Leamer and others censure him merely for his possible thoughts and fantasies. One wonders if the ungainly Hitchcock had the dashing good looks of Victor Fleming or the machismo of John Huston or the merely passable countenances of any of the other lotharios who flourished in Hollywood, would he be scapegoated so harshly?

Leamer tells us that "He had a daughter and three grandchildren, yet he sounded as if children were an exotic species unknown to him" (248). By all accounts and photographic evidence, Hitchcock was a doting paterfamilias, and in raising Patricia Hitchcock he might have invented "Take Your Daughter to Work Day." We can see for ourselves the warmth exuded in the father-daughter relationships in many of the films and how they point to an appreciation for those relationships. Adding that Hitchcock thought of children as "one of life's minor afflictions" (249), Leamer contradicts that thought by quoting Veronica Cartwright's extremely fond recollection of her time on *The Birds* and her lovely relationship with the director.

Chief among the many women in the Hitchcock orbit (outside of Alma) was Joan Harrison, who rose in his office from secretary to screenwriter to producer, and was a valued friend and confidante. Leamer is quick to point out that foremost among her qualifications was being a sophisticated blonde. Spoto goes through some serious gymnastics in an effort to contort the possibility of some sort of sexual intrigue between the two but can't quite twist it into believability.

Under Hitchcock's fostering, Harrison eventually branched out as an estimable producer in her own right—in 1943 the *New York Times* called her "Hollywood's only full-fledged woman producer" (48).

Leamer, who acknowledges that "In so many Hitchcock films, the female lead is the strongest character" (66), credits Harrison for giving us, in her first film, the terrific *Phantom Lady* (1944, directed by Robert Siodmak), a "female heroine" (is there any other kind?) unique in Hollywood films at the time. Carol, the protagonist in *Phantom Lady*, is a secretary in love with her boss. When he is charged with the murder of his wife, she sets out to prove his innocence. Leamer describes Carol as "honest, bold, and truthful" (48), which, redundancy aside, puts her right in the mold of the heroines Hitchcock had been giving us for years. What Leamer doesn't note is the distinct difference between Carol and the women of Hitchcock. Carol, for all her pluck and persistence, is driven solely by romantic love. She doesn't develop as Hitchcock heroines do by finding their place in the larger world. She is the same at the end as she was in the beginning (wonderful but unchanged) and her ultimate reward for her loyalty and initiative is that she lands her man.

Compare Carol to her precedent, Iris Henderson in *The Lady Vanishes* (1938). Iris, after feeling she has done everything there is to do in her frivolous life, is now blandly on her way to a loveless marriage, because that is what one does. What she makes happen on that trip—and she makes it happen, it doesn't happen to her—saving the life of a woman, and in effect, maybe saving the world, shows her that she can go beyond "what one does." She finds there are other ways to live a life, with true love dropping in as a fringe benefit. Charlie Newton, Pat Martin, Connie Porter, Alicia Huberman, Juanita de Cordoba, Eve Kendall, Jo McKenna, Carol Fisher— they all play critical parts beyond their own personal lives and learn about themselves in the process. Whether as local or international heroines, the stakes for the women in Hitchcock are sky-high, going way beyond romantic love. These characters never come out the same as they went in. That

Hitchcock recognized and launched a smart, independent woman like Harrison into success should alone make one question the intimations of misogyny that bedevil his reputation. That he had been creating heroines just as—if not more—"honest, bold, and truthful" as she, should wipe out those whiffs of woman-hating completely.

Part of Leamer's problem in writing about Hitchcock is that he takes everything the man has said out loud at face value—just as he suggested Tippi Hedren mistakenly did. He makes an absurd statement such as "Like most men of his generation he thought women had their place, but it was not out in the world doing things men do" because Hitch once quipped "Would you expect a girls' school to be built by girls?" (28). If there is anything one learns in studying Hitchcock, it is not to pay too much heed to some of the silly things that he says. From characterizing actors as livestock to blithe remarks on torturing women, he knew how to get a rise out of his audience. The fellow was above all, and always, a showman. And because he was always encrusted in character, we don't really know what he thought or felt about anything beyond filmmaking. His ear was forever out for the laugh, the gasp, the scream.

Leamer sets out to illustrate Hitchcock's offenses but his book is so loaded with contradictions and backtracking that he never makes a convincing argument. His interviews with living actors Eva Marie Saint and Kim Novak not only add no fuel to that fire, they douse it. Donald Spoto, try as he might, had a hard time finding any actress who expressed resentment of Hitchcock's methods, which he rationalized as likely because his films were good for their careers. Even he had to grudgingly acknowledge the affection most of them felt for the man, such as Alida Valli's deep gratitude for his kindness to an actress in a strange land or his protective care for young Nova Pilbeam. When Spoto failed to land any disparaging commentary from Eva Marie Saint amid her merry memories of making *North by Northwest,* he closes that chapter with disappointment dripping from his pen as he writes her off as "docile and cooperative."[13]

In his shaky conviction of Hitchcock's maltreatment of women, Leamer offers this outlandish conjecture:

> [Women] repeatedly returned to the movies to see members of their sex abused in Hitchcock's films. Some of these women had inchoate anger about themselves and their lives that they played out on screen. Others took pleasure in watching women being put through some savage tests. (12)

It's a preposterous deduction that might offend not only Hitchcock defenders but any woman who goes to the movies. Yes, women do go through some things in Hitchcock films (as do men, as do the protagonists in about every story ever told), but what Leamer is missing and what is so striking is that we see what she goes through from her perspective.

From *Blackmail* (1929) to *Psycho* to *Marnie* (1964) to *Frenzy* (1972), scenes of visceral attacks are shown from the woman's point of view. Alice White in *Blackmail* fights back and kills her attacker, and we are all for it; the loss of Marion Crane hits us so hard because up to that point in the film, we have traveled with her, hoping she would see the light, and then when she does, it's too late; some have pointed to the rape in *Marnie* as some kind of endorsement of a husband assuming his marital right, rather than the shameful act that leads to a suicide attempt; *Frenzy* presents rape as something completely unromantic and horrible perpetrated not on a sex object but a middle-aged working woman with whom we identify until her last breath. The pleasure we get watching these scenes are not from any prurient joy of watching women suffer, as Leamer propounds, but recognition of the artistry in conveying the nightmares that women are all too familiar with.

A wide range of lechery and male menace are depicted in Hitchcock films, quite bluntly and always from the female perspective. In *The Paradine Case* (1947), Gay Keane's disgust is palpable as the gruesome Judge Horfield salivates over her; in *Psycho*, we can feel with Marion the "hot-as-fresh-milk" breath of the goatish Mr. Cassidy on her "fine, soft flesh"; in *Rear Window* (1954), both Miss Torso and Miss Lonelyhearts—two very different women who are living alone—manage to shut the door on men who we can plainly see don't want to take "no" for an answer. Not only are we put in the shoes of these beleaguered women, but in every case—with perhaps the exception of the not-so-confident Miss Lonelyhearts—they dodge these reptilian Romeos with aplomb.

There is no better example of female forbearance than the hotel lobby scene in *Spellbound* (1945). Constance Petersen sits alone, minding her own business, when a liquored-up lug oafishly moves in on her. The hotel detective intervenes, chasing the pest away, even though she was managing fine on her own. The detective himself proves to be rather ambiguous in his intrusive manner, asking her personal questions as if being a woman alone in a public place is somehow suspicious. She can't tell if he's trying to be helpful or harassing, and neither can we, but she quick-wittedly finesses him to get her the information she's after. I don't think there is a woman alive who doesn't relate to her situation, even if we don't always handle it as masterfully as Dr. Peterson. The beauty of the women in Hitchcock comes not in blondeness but in their cleverness, their way of deftly eluding objectification, and their ability to fend for themselves.

And that applies to the women who played them as well. Blonde or brunette, the women who worked with Hitchcock did not have to be rescued—not by Donald Spoto, not by Lawrence Leamer, nor any chivalrous male writers who depict these women as victims of Hitchcock's supposed "sadism" or manipulations. Leamer seems to want to press the idea that Hitchcock took advantage of female disadvantage, but what he actually shows us are women who were as worldly and self-sufficient as *Lifeboat's* (1944) Connie Porter, with impressive careers and independent lives. They knew how to take care of themselves. As Jay Presson Allen observed, Hitchcock liked women who could stand up to him (259). As audacious as he could be, he appreciated audacity in women. He never had use for damsels in distress—and yet the authors of these books keep looking for them. If only they could give as much credence to women as Hitchcock did.

Reading *Hitchcock's Blondes*, one might come away still asking was Hitchcock so inappropriate that he verged on the monstrous? In Leamer's hands he comes off as being perhaps pathological in his impropriety but not quite the evil monster that Spoto presents.[14] In her self-examination of her own response to art-monsters in her book *Monsters: A Fans's Dilemma*, Claire Dederer, in writing about artists she adores but who behave badly, wonders about the "absoluteness of monstrosity and absoluteness of genius."[15] Dederer does not include Hitchcock in her rogue's gallery that includes a wide spectrum of scoundrels from a convicted rapist to mere garden variety narcissists. Perhaps Hitchcock doesn't register as relevant to her discussion because by her metrics his alleged offenses don't warrant inclusion or it could be that she's just not into Hitchcock as genius. But she could certainly be referring to the depictions Leamer and others have drawn when she writes:

> They were accused of doing or saying something awful, and they made something great. The awful thing disrupts the great work without remembering the awful thing. Flooded with knowledge of the maker's monstrousness, we turn away, overcome by disgust or . . . we don't. We continue watching, separating or trying to separate the artist from the art. Either way: disruption.[16]

Personally, outside of fiction, I don't believe in monsters. And the storied monsters I've read about, from Caliban to Frankenstein's creation to King Kong, I love and embrace as figures who inspire magnificent sympathy. I also reject the notion of "evil," which strikes me as both a lazy and arcane explanation of the motives of our worst actions. The cry of "Evil!" as heard in the insane shriek of a hysterical mother in *The Birds*, does nothing but shut down any exploration of the human condition.

My own aversion to the "monster" epithet might have come from Hitchcock himself. For when Hitchcock served up souls who were rotten and beyond redemption, he presented them with nuance and a bit of understanding. He discerned that every one of us is a mixed bag: Alexander Sebastian is a devoted and loving husband. Stephen Fisher is a good father and, in the end, a hero. Norman Bates is a most misunderstood murderer. Charles Oakley is a beloved brother and the victim of a childhood accident. Rico Parra is a confounding concoction of righteousness and malevolence. It is kidnapper Mrs. Drayton who tells us "It doesn't hurt to be kind"—and she means it. We never know the motives of the birds but we are ready to believe that perhaps those winged revolutionaries just had enough with being shot at, baked, broiled, and fried.

Many of us can accept that great art doesn't have to come from a flawless creator. Just how defective Hitchcock was remains unknown, because the man kept himself hidden, as was his right. But the dead are often laid out to have their lives picked over and plundered by biographers and by those advancing their own agendas in memoirs. Some of Hitchcock's less admirable traits are well-established: the crude jokes; that he was not effusive with praise; that he was sadly ungenerous when giving credit to colleagues; and that in realizing his vision he could be oblivious to some of the ordeals he put actors through. In spite of the specious scavenging by Spoto and Leamer, that is all we really know, and it renders a debate on Hitchcock's character based on biographers' presumptions futile.

The art of Alfred Hitchcock, however, is fair game for argument and certainly the films invite us to speculate about the man who made them. Interpretations are going to vary— some see a woman relentlessly stabbed in a shower or pecked apart by birds and they cluck their tongues and shake their heads and contend that the man who could imagine such things must hate women. Others can watch the same footage and see a couple of complex and venturesome women—yes, in these cases, blondes—who get in their cars and drive the action. Sure, they suffer (well, in *The Birds*, everyone suffers—women, men, children, and horses) but through their experiences we see them wake up to a new consciousness, even if for Marion Crane it is tragically too late. As passionately as these views can be disputed, if we stick to the work, it will at least elevate the discussion of Hitchcock the human being beyond gossipy innuendo.

By emphasizing Hitchcock's supposed blonde obsession, Leamer amplifies the myth of the man's misogyny and at the same time promotes the stereotype of his heroines as icy blonde sirens when in fact they were so much more. And it's not only his leading ladies but their supporting sisters as well who come on their scenes with richness and dimension. Even young Cathy Brenner in *The Birds* proves to be a Hitchcock heroine in training. She's valiant enough to help a fallen classmate in the midst of an attack and humane enough to rescue the caged lovebirds with the simple reasoning that "They haven't hurt anyone." And, incidentally, it is Alfred Hitchcock—the presumed perv, the creep, the evil monster—who gives us that moment of exquisite tenderness. It is he, the one whose lack of empathy is cited in *Hitchcock's Blondes*, reminding us that we are capable of forgiveness, tolerance, and compassion.

I suspect that at least some of those who judge Hitchcock so stringently are condemning him not solely for his treatment of women on screen or off but maybe for telling us more about ourselves than we want to know. In Hitchcock we confront the good with the not so nice parts of who we are. For we have all made bad decisions, behaved inappropriately, and have caused suffering at one time or another. We all likely harbor glints of perversity. We all go a little mad sometimes. I don't mean to brush off accusations against Hitchcock with a "nobody's perfect" shrug and leave it at that. But I do think we can all gain something from Hitchcock's understanding of human nature. He puts out the troublesome prospect that in every regular Guy lurks a disturbed Bruno. There is hardly a character—man or woman—who gets by him unblemished: Charlie Newton lies to her friend and laughs about it. Blanche

Tyler is a con artist. L.B. Jefferies is a peeping Tom. Melanie Daniels is a heedless hedonist. Devlin is prejudiced. Francie Stevens is spoiled. Connie Porter is solipsistic. Margot Wendice is unfaithful. Scottie Ferguson is neurotic. Richard Blaney is just plain unlikeable. These twists of humanity are at the very marrow of Hitchcock's work where he is able to deliver the thing that eludes both Leamer and Spoto: that the imponderabilia of a life, of a person's character, is not something that can be so easily evaluated. Because, if you look hard enough, in every little lamb you will find a spot.

Notes

I am deeply grateful for the always insightful and supreme editorial counsel of Sidney Gottlieb.

1. Donald Spoto, *The Dark Side of Genius* (Boston: Little, Brown, 1983).

2. Donald Spoto, *Spellbound by Beauty: Alfred Hitchcock and His Leading Ladies* (New York: Harmony Books, 2008).

3. *The Girl*, directed by Julian Jarrold (HBO Films, 2012).

4. Elisabeth Karlin, "Beyond the Blonde: The Dynamic Heroines of Hitchcock," *Hitchcock Annual* 25 (2021): 32-55.

5. Lawrence Leamer, *Capote's Women* (New York: G.P. Putnam's Sons, 2021); *Feud: Capote vs. The Swans*, directed by Gus Van Sant *et al.* (FX, 2024).

6. Donald Spoto, *The Art of Alfred Hitchcock: Fifty Years of his Motion Pictures* (New York: Hopkinson and Blake, 1976), xi. I should mention here that my father edited and published this book. I read it first as a manuscript that I couldn't put down, and I will be forever indebted to Donald Spoto for opening my eyes to a new way of seeing Hitchcock.

7. Spoto, *Spellbound by Beauty*, 16.

8. Laurence Leamer, *Hitchcock's Blondes: The Unforgettable Women Behind the Legendary Director's Dark Obsession* (New York: G.P. Putnam's Sons, 2023), 11. All quotations from this book will be cited by page number only in the text of my essay.

9. Hitchcock wasn't the only twentieth-century genius who came under fire for his relationships with the women he worked with. Like Hitchcock, Russian George Balanchine also emigrated to

the U.S. in the 1930s to become the most influential choreographer in America. The striking parallels between the two include attacks on Balanchine for his idealization of the female body and how that influenced dancers to starve themselves. Late in life, his fixation on ballerina Suzanne Farrell came to a bad juncture when she married another dancer and he had her dismissed from the New York City Ballet. The difference between his object of obsession and Hitchcock's though is stark. Suzanne Farrell was probably the greatest dancer of her generation, a claim that Tippi Hedren could hardly make as an actress. Also, Farrell and Balanchine did reconcile.

10. Greg Garrett, "Hitchcock's Women on Hitchcock: A Panel Discussion with Janet Leigh, Tippi Hedren, Karen Black, Suzanne Pleshette, and Eva Marie Saint," *Literature/Film Quarterly* 27, no. 2 (1999): 278-89.

11. Quoted in Tony Lee Moral, *Hitchcock and the Making of Marnie* (Lanham, MD: Scarecrow Press, 2005), 120.

12. Tippi Hedren, panel on *The Girl, The Wrap*, August 1, 2012, online at www.thewrap.com/tippi-hedren-hitchcock-genius-and-evil-and-deviant-almost-point-dangerous-50391/

13. Spoto, *Spellbound by Beauty*, 188.

14. In spite of their being shades of Donald Spoto's influence in the "dark obsession" that Leamer leans into, he never mentions him by name in the text, only as a "Hitchcock biographer" (270).

15. Clare Dederer, *Monsters: A Fan's Dilemma* (New York: Alfred A. Knopf, 2023), 14.

16. Clare Dederer, *Monsters*, 23.

DAVID STERRITT

Antiquity, Taxidermy, and Two Hitchcock Classics

Mark William Padilla, *Classical Vertigo: Mythic Shapes and Contemporary Influences in Hitchcock's Film*. Lanham, MD: Lexington Books, 2024. xvii + 319 pp. $125.00 cloth, $45.00 ebook.

Subarna Mondal. *Alfred Hitchcock's Psycho and Taxidermy: Fashioning Corpses*. New York: Bloomsbury Academic, 2024. ix + 154 pp. $70.00 cloth, $63.00 ebook.

Critics, scholars, and cinephiles may never stop devising new ways to explore Alfred Hitchcock's endlessly explorable films. The question thus becomes whether the bottomless well of fresh interpretations is yielding an ongoing wealth of worthwhile ideas, or whether novelty is sometimes being valued, or overvalued, for its own sake. Recent examples suggest a mixed verdict. *Classical Vertigo: Mythic Shapes and Contemporary Influences in Hitchcock's Film* was written by Mark William Padilla, who has been tracing "shapes of antiquity" in Hitchcock's work in books and articles since the early 2010s; he acknowledges that some might regard his single-minded pursuit as "a bit fetishistic in nature," but he likens himself to "an archaeologist working at an important ancient city" and contends that classicism is a robust means of addressing the "creative sources and drives" that power the director's work. This is his first lengthy book devoted to a single Hitchcock film. Subarna Mondal's monograph *Alfred Hitchcock's Psycho and Taxidermy: Fashioning Corpses* also examines a single key film from a singular vantage point, but its perspective is more bounded, aiming to trade familiar theoretical frameworks— "historicist, feminist psychoanalytic, Marxist"—for a focus on the materiality and physicality of Hitchcock's "most prominently corporeal Gothic film." Both books look at notably specialized aspects of Hitchcock's cinema.

Although mythologies from the ancient world are the primary intertexts in *Classical Vertigo*, a pair of more recent works also figure prominently in Padilla's ambitious study. One is, unsurprisingly, the 1954 novel *D'Entre les morts* by Pierre Boileau and Thomas Narcejac. Published in English as *The Living and the Dead* in 1956, this became a basic source of the screenplay for *Vertigo* (1958) by Samuel A. Taylor and Alec Coppel, who altered the tale with Hitchcock's ideas in mind. Padilla sees certain "mythic motifs" as key links between the novel and film, such as the story of Orpheus, who journeys into the underworld to retrieve his beloved Eurydice after her death, much as Scottie Ferguson moves through an increasingly dreamlike San Francisco in search of Madeleine Elster, the mysterious woman who appears to have killed herself during their initial acquaintance. These resemblances are not hard to spot, and Padilla underscores how they enrich the film; the same goes for his detailed examinations of other mythic figures indirectly adduced in *Vertigo*—Prometheus and Pandora, Io and Argos, Hades and Persephone—as well as the Golden Bough, the Golden Fleece, and other talismanic objects. He also digs into structural traits of ancient dramatic literature and treatments of mythological material by the playwrights Sophocles and Aeschylus, the poets Ovid and Vergil, and more. Padilla displays impressive knowledge in all these areas.

The other modern literary work he explores at length is Georges Rodenbach's 1892 novel *Bruges-la-Morte*, notable for its embodiment of Symbolist aesthetics and for its innovative use of photographs placed strategically throughout the text. Its protagonist is a grieving widower whose home in Bruges is filled with letters, clothing, and other items associated with his late wife. Wandering through the lonely streets and decaying architecture of the "dead city," which uncannily mirror his own melancholic daze, his life is dominated by mournful memories until he has a chance encounter with a beautiful dancer who resembles his late wife so uncannily that he becomes obsessed with her, realizing too belatedly that her personality is the opposite of what he had hoped. The parallels between *Bruges-la-Morte* and both *D'Entre les morts* and *Vertigo* are inexact but striking, and Padilla argues that Hitchcock's sensibility was highly receptive to the Symbolist orientation of Rodenbach's book. If the Boileau-Narcejac novel "served as the birth mother of the film," he writes, "*Bruges-la-Morte* sired it," and even though Boileau-Narcejac provided Hitchcock with "a source of plot mechanics and narrative details," the Rodenbach book has a more "profound aesthetic and psychological kinship" with the film. Padilla's analysis of affinities between Hitchcock and Rodenbach fills many of his most useful pages.

Other pages are less successful, however. The book digresses from its main arguments in ways that are not always persuasive, often leaving *Vertigo* behind for meandering excursions into fuzzily outlined details of Boileau-Narcejac territory. Padilla argues, for instance, that "references and allusions to ancient Rome and its imperial actions serve as a programmatic theme" in *D'Entre les morts*, and to support this he cites such particulars as the "Roman features" of certain characters and the "Gallo-Roman" ruins in a village near the site of Madeleine's ostensible suicide; he also contends that Boileau and Narcejac deploy "long-held biases about Roman versus Greek sensibilities, such as pragmatism versus heroic emotion," to characterize the personalities of Flavières and Gévigne, the novel's Scottie and Elster prototypes. These notions may be true, but it's a long way from there to the specifics of Hitchcock's film. A loose and uncertain structure is a recurring weakness in *Classical Vertigo*.

The book also pays close attention to Hitchcock collaborators whose creative contributions have received limited analysis from earlier scholars. One of them is Maxwell Anderson, the hugely versatile writer—by Padilla's count he wrote more than forty dramas, musicals, and radio plays, some produced and others not—enlisted by Hitchcock to pen the screenplay for *The Wrong Man* (1956), which was subsequently revised by Angus MacPhail, and then to write an adaptation of *D'Entre les morts*, which Hitchcock promptly rejected. Anderson was indeed an estimable author, with such significant stage plays as *Winterset* (1935, film directed by Alfred Santell in 1936) and *The Bad Seed* (1954, film directed by Mervyn LeRoy in 1956) among his credits. But this part of Padilla's book suffers from his tendency to develop questionable and sometimes far-fetched connections among works that are distantly related at best. With respect to Anderson, he acknowledges that it is "of course counter-intuitive to think about *Vertigo* as influenced substantively by an uncredited writer," and then proceeds to spend no fewer than eighty pages linking Anderson with Hitchcock, arguing (among other things) that Anderson's ability "to evolve as a writer to tackle new kinds of projects" provided Hitchcock with a "model" for "his own decision in the mid-1950s to "create Hollywood movies that engaged more European sensibilities," as if Hitchcock needed a "model" to inspire his work of that amazing decade.

Examining ties between Hitchcock and Anderson is certainly worthwhile, but Padilla resorts to uncomfortably strained logic, as a couple of examples illustrate. He writes that Howard Hawks's *To Have and Have Not* (1944) is based on an Anderson play, that it was the first of four films to pair Humphrey Bogart and Lauren Bacall, and that such important authors as Ernest Hemingway and William Faulkner worked on some of the screenplays; this is all accurate, but he goes on to suggest that these "high-status-author and high-status-director projects" propelled Hitchcock to employ Anderson for *Vertigo*, implying that Anderson was somehow an auteur of all four films and that Hitchcock was more a follower of fashion than a uniquely original artist. The latter implication also arises when Padilla notes Anderson's love of "the sea and water bodies in general" and claims that "it is possible that the water motifs in *Vertigo* stem from this influence." Almost anything is possible, of course, but could not Hitchcock's watery moments have been his own ideas? In another flight of interpretive fancy, Padilla recalls the scandal surrounding Ingrid Bergman's affair with the neorealist director Roberto Rossellini and temporary exit from Hollywood, and suggests that *Vertigo* may have been Hitchcock's attempt at "willing" her back to America's attention while worrying about whether audiences would receive her "as the lower-class Judy figure from *Stromboli* or the elegant Madeleine from the Hitchcockian concoctions of Constance in *Spellbound*, Alicia in *Notorious*, and Henrietta in *Under Capricorn*." All of this arises from Padilla's observation that a play by Anderson was the basis for Victor Fleming's 1948 epic *Joan of Arc*, released to considerable controversy just as Bergman's relationship with Rossellini was becoming public knowledge, and Padilla oddly speculates that Hitchcock's ruminations on her travails played an influential role in the shaping of *Vertigo*. He also states that Bergman's "shocking abandonment of Hollywood and her family" to work with Rossellini in Italy was what "triggered" the neorealist look of *The Wrong Man*, adding that Hitchcock perhaps wanted "to impress Bergman and soothe his jilted ego with the style of the film, given his attraction to her charms." Hitchcock's attraction to the charms of leading ladies is well known, but the notion of *The Wrong Man* as a veiled plea for Bergman's affection is hard to credit.

Other connections posited by Padilla also seem tenuous to the vanishing point. Instances abound in his discussion of *Vertigo* and Hitchcock's minor opus *Waltzes from Vienna*, the "adapted operatic musical" released in 1934. After correctly noting that *Bruges-la-Morte* was the basis for Erich Wolfgang Korngold's dark-toned 1920 opera *Die tote Stadt*, Padilla goes on to link all three of the earlier works—the Hitchcock film, the Rodenbach novel, and the Korngold opera—with *Vertigo*, using Bernard Herrmann's score for *Vertigo* as a bridge. Herrmann's score plays an exceptionally important role in *Vertigo*, to be sure, and Padilla aptly quotes Hitchcock's famous comment about the Empire Hotel scene where Judy emerges in full Madeleine regalia: "We should let all traffic noises fade, because Mr. Herrmann may have something to say here." But this doesn't mean Hitchcock approached the film "in part in the fashion of a libretto-and-score design," as Padilla claims, or that Herrmann himself "signals" this structure with musical references to Richard Wagner's operas *Tristan und Isolde* and *Die Walküre*, operas that Padilla calls "a direct influence" on Richard Strauss II, the central character in *Waltzes from Vienna*. All this amounts to a very strained way of linking *Vertigo* and *Waltzes from Vienna*, films that really couldn't be more different, and Padilla hardly strengthens the argument by pointing out that in his *Vertigo* cameo Hitchcock is holding a musical-instrument case, or that Judy and Midge in *Vertigo* and Strauss's love interest in *Waltzes from Vienna* all "work in non-domestic jobs." It's also worth remembering that while *Vertigo* is a masterpiece, Hitchcock told François Truffaut that *Waltzes from Vienna* was "very bad," a judgment generally shared by moviegoers.

Finally, brief mention must be made of minor errors scattered through the book. Howard Hawks and *Swann's Way* are misspelled; Robert Graves is renamed Michael; John Ford is credited with directing Fred Zinnemann's *Oklahoma!* (1955). And in the course of praising *Vertigo*, Padilla uses its 1996 restoration as evidence of its lasting worthiness, which is a needless gesture, since film restoration has become an industry and plenty of inconsequential works have benefited from it. Readers interested in the classical undertones of Hitchcock's cinema will find much to think about in *Classical Vertigo*. But one wishes Padilla could come up with an alternate cut that hewed more intently to its main concerns and held back the impulse to forge shaky connections among distantly related facts and factoids. That would be a more valuable contribution to Hitchcock studies.

As she notes in her Preface, Mondal conceived and developed *Alfred Hitchcock's Psycho and Taxidermy* while coping with a series of personal injuries and illnesses, regrettable but appropriate conditions for writing a "book with the body at its center." Tapping into the tradition of nineteenth-century

Gothic literature, which purposefully disturbs "the reassuring lines between familiar and unfamiliar, fantasy and nightmare, progression and regression," she makes the very good point that taxidermy, like the far stranger activities recounted in such works as H.G. Wells's *The Island of Dr. Moreau* (1896), Robert Louis Stevenson's *The Strange Case of Dr. Jekyll and Mr. Hyde* (1886), and Arthur Machen's *The Great God Pan* (1894), represents an attempt "to achieve wholeness and stability with raw materials (the skin and the body) that are themselves given to fragmentation and permeability." Seeking permanency in the impermanent, a taxidermist may be called "a speculator in perishables," a phrase Hitchcock has used to describe himself. Norman Bates could have appropriated it as well: "Art that deals with hollow structures and dead skin that look alive," Mondal writes, "is a perfect art for a man with a hollow life, a life that he seeks to stuff with the skin of his mother." This ably captures Norman and his hobby.

Mondal likens the moribund Mrs. Bates to the many "aberrant bodies" kept in Victorian houses, cellars, and attics in such literary works as Charlotte Brontë's *Jane Eyre* (1847), Emily Brontë's *Wuthering Heights* (1847), Charles Dickens's *Great Expectations* (1861), and Bram Stoker's *Dracula* (1897). Mondal also connects her with the preserved animal cadavers that fascinated Victorian England, a milieu that greatly influenced Hitchcock, as Paula Marantz Cohen and other film scholars have shown. Mondal's explications of taxidermy focus primarily on Victorian practices, but she extends her frame of reference by discussing links between taxidermy and present-day issues of sexism and speciesism. "The manufacturing of a 'docile' body," she explains, "performing and posing in accordance to the whims of its maker, and, in the process, incarcerating the maker in the unpredicted outcome of his craft," is a complex activity that joins speciesism to sexism and makes both implicit elements of Hitchcock's film.

She also discusses how Hitchcock's technical trickery—deploying body doubles and other counterfeits to concoct the visuals of Mrs. Bates, using multiple male and female voices to provide her spoken words—makes the character a "Re-Creation," a term used by taxidermists for "renderings which include no natural parts of the animal portrayed." Most entertainingly, she delves into the peculiar precincts of "rogue taxidermy" and "crap taxidermy," overlapping domains dedicated to "freak specimens of nonhumans engaged in highly eccentric human gestures." Norman has much in common with the rogues, Mondal contends, and his mother might belong in the crap category, given her resemblance to a freak-show figure.

Mondal uses such groupings judiciously, keeping the spotlight on taxidermy rather than taxonomy. She is also judicious in her assessments of Hitchcock's films, proffering much praise but not hesitating to be critical, as when she calls *Frenzy* (1972) a "sloppy" story with numerous narrative "loopholes" made by a director "not much concerned with the technicalities of crime detection" but very concerned with "the staging of naked dead women." Yet she suggests that *Frenzy* as a whole reveals "a direct link between the physical brutality meted out to women and the rampant institutional misogyny within the legal system," and this goes some way toward justifying its cinematic excesses. Other films also enter Mondal's picture, including the 1956 version of Hitchcock's own *The Man Who Knew Too Much*, where the memorable scene in Ambrose Chappell's taxidermy shop was shot in a London taxidermist's actual establishment, and such later works as Jonathan Demme's *The Silence of the Lambs* (1991) and Pedro Almodóvar's *The Skin I Live In* (2011). A few minor films with taxidermy elements are mentioned as well, including György Pálfi's *Taxidermia* (2006) and José Rammon Larraz's *Deviation* (1971), but the taxidermy scenes in those movies are few and fleeting, confirming once again that *Psycho* is the crowning work in this curious subgenre.

Filmmakers themselves might be called speculators in perishables, since motion pictures truly exist only as their light flashes across the screen, but books like *Classical Vertigo* and *Alfred Hitchcock's Psycho and Taxidermy* keep movies alive in different forms. Both volumes travel into the cultural past, with Padilla taking a sprawling, sometimes almost free-associative approach, tying together people and films in ways ranging from ingenious to implausible, and Mondal building a more closely bound set of arguments in a more succinct manner. Although the books are geared to hard-core Hitchcockians rather than cinephiles at large, they should interest any reader looking for offbeat perspectives on two of the auteur's most justly celebrated films.

Rod Stoneman

The Afterlife of the Auteur:
My Name is Alfred Hitchcock

My Name is Alfred Hitchcock, Mark Cousins's recent essay film, is an original and creative deconstruction of Hitchcock's movies and, in a wider sense of "Hitchcock," the meanings, connotations, and concepts that cluster around the authorial or *auteurial* persona. Cousins proposes inventive tools for understanding individual films and the *oeuvre* as a whole. His essayistic assertions are provocative and catalytic. Crucially, his film takes the fascinations, without dwelling on the problematic issues that have been raised over the years about Hitchcock's work, to a wider and non-academic audience, playing across many of the frames in which Hitchcock's films are held at the present time.

I

Hitchcock was one of the first directors to become an authorial brand for a wide popular cinema-going public, following Cecil B. DeMille and D.W. Griffith, whose films were literally signed, whose names labelled their cinema, and Chaplin who established himself in front of and behind the camera. Hitchcock carefully fashioned a persona and made it visible in the text itself with witty cameo appearances in many of the films. The signatory presence of the director suggests, like speech, that the named subject is present and talking to you directly, rather than an abstract and sometimes absent author behind a piece of writing or a standard Hollywood film. Hitchcock's consciousness of overtly presenting himself is the implicit context for Cousins to be able to both elaborate and hypothesize the persona further.

By this stage in cultural history, Hitchcock's work has become the definitive representative of classical Hollywood in the popular imagination. Younger generations have a changing relation to the echoes of historical forms of cinema that they generally experience through black and white images, which, in commodity culture, hold connotations of the rare and the stylish. This is the new framework that allows Cousins's essay film, using samples of Hitchcock's original images, many in black and white, to take on novel and nuanced meanings. His insertion of shots of contemporary viewers and locations from the films as well as Hitchcock's famed profile emphasizes the transferral of the reading of Hitchcock to a new place and time and the presence of a new presumed audience.

Made between a century and a half-a-century ago, Hitchcock's films occupy a very different place in the contemporary image system than when they were produced—placed amongst the continuously flowing pixels and their new color variants, with better sound technology, configurations, amongst faster-paced image streams often interrupted by advertising, and generally viewed on different sized screens. In some cases this heightens and in other cases diminishes the audio and visual quality of the films.[1] Hitchcock's films, including those with saturated color like *Vertigo* (1958) and *Marnie* (1964), as well as the black and white of *I Confess* (1953) and *Psycho* (1960), are now coded as "art" and exhibited in those specific spaces within cinemas, television, and streaming. In these changed viewing conditions, they are of course still "readable" by a wide audience as examples of compelling, powerful cinema. In over a hundred years, industrial, commercial filmmaking has evolved, but still there is an underlying continuity in the operation of its narrative structures and the spectator's positioning in this process; it can be said that contemporary codes of representation inhabit a paradoxical relation to earlier cinema as "the same but different."

While making movies in the epoch before Film Studies was constructed and institutionalized, Hitchcock emerged as one of "the greatest directors of all time"; this took place exactly alongside the growth of serious writing about film during the period where "film appreciation" merged into "film criticism," following the influence of figures associated with *Cahiers du Cinéma* (most notably Eric Rohmer, Claude Chabrol, and François Truffaut) and the impact of *Movie* and *Screen* in the Anglophone sphere.[2]

Hitchcock was placed in the category of "Pantheon Directors" in Andrew Sarris's *The American Cinema* as the Anglophone version of the auteur theory was established, and the position of *Vertigo* in the *Slight and Sound* ten best lists over the years has perpetuated his status for cinephiles.[3] Twenty-five years after his death, Hitchcock is ensured a consolidated place in academic structures, as the proliferation of conferences and indeed the very existence of a journal like the *Hitchcock Annual* indicates. The academic industry has an insatiable need for new material and new sub-disciplines, and "Hitchcock Studies" has been central to many evolving debates on semiotics and psychoanalysis, feminism, and gender. A few years ago, archivists at the Motion Picture Association of America complained of the "relentless demands for material from our collections to be included in Hitchcock exhibitions. . . . they don't seem so interested in the other directors of that time."[4] At this period of such interest in Hitchcock and the continued profusion of material about him, Cousins's film is distinct, with sufficient inventiveness of form and literally freshness of voice to make a valuable addition.

The attention to Hitchcock often involves his own endorsement and authorization of the meaning of the films. An interesting and contrasting authorial viewpoint can be found in the visual arts: in "The Creative Act," a talk he gave in 1957, Marcel Duchamp argued that the generation of meaning for a work of art is determined less by author's intention than by the spectator's interpretation.[5] Despite Roland Barthes declaring the "death of the author" in the early 1960s (soon to be followed by Michel Foucault and many others), the cult of the author remains central to the ideologies of *cinephilia* and wider versions of culture in the West. We unconsciously expect the meaning of the artwork (film, visual arts, or literature) to be framed by biographical discourse and connected with some aspects of the author's life and preoccupations. Whether assumed or projected, historically accurate or recently imagined, the artist's (generally understood as a single determinate individual) behavior and attitudes are conscripted in the construction of interpretation. As Barthes describes it, "the explanation of the work is still sought in the person of its producer."[6]

There is the unstated absence of the author, for instance, when we encounter Palaeographic murals or Roman statues that cannot be encased in presupposition connecting their makers.[7] It is interesting that in relatively recent revelations from Sumerian archaeology the poet Enheduanna, the first named writer in human history, was a woman we know virtually nothing about, other than the bare facts that she was a poet and priestess who lived in Mesopotamia in 2300 B.C.[8] Written over 4000 years ago, her poetry stands without attached knowledge about its creator.[9]

In Hitchcock's case, his unremarkable personal life throws the auteurist focus back on the texts he fashioned, and Hitchcock himself was careful to resist being drawn into an explanation of *what they really mean*. Successive *Cahiers du Cinéma* critics found consistent underlying meaning in his films, projecting concepts of Jansenist guilt (which may say more about the analyzers than the analysed). For example, André Bazin's 1954 interview with Hitchcock in Cannes confronted him with these interpretations: "While traditional criticism often reproaches you for brilliant but gratuitous formalism several young French critics, on the contrary, profess a nearly universal admiration for your work and discover, beyond the detective story, a constant and profound message."[10] Hitchcock refuted this suggestion with an avowal of profound formalism: "I am interested not so much in the stories I tell as in the means of telling them." This stratagem emerges again in Truffaut's book-length interview, and there

Figure 1

is the sense that, whether intentional or not, the filmmaker is investing in the longer-term life of his work by refusing to add his imprimatur with definitive intention to one set of interpretive meanings.[11] The displacement to a focus on form works to reinforce the enduring polysemic potential of the films themselves.

It is significant that much of the first serious consideration of Hitchcock came from critics who were also filmmakers—Truffaut, Chabrol, Rohmer, Jacques Rivette, and Jean-Luc Godard. Hitchcock's films have increasingly become the starting point for artists' filmmaking: an inventive catalyst generating new experimental films screened in art galleries. The use of Hitchcock films by Douglas Gordon, Pierre Huyghe, Johan Grimonprez, Matthias Müller, and Christoph Giradet has taken his work to an art context.[12]

Johan Grimonprez's *Double Take* (2009) casts Alfred Hitchcock as a paranoid history professor (fig. 1), unwittingly caught up in the media-generated myths circulating during the Cold War period. The "double take" is a second thought suggesting that both cinema and political ideology trade in the same "fear as a commodity."[13]

In "Why Don't You Love Me?," a nine-minute section of Matthias Müller and Christoph Giradet's *Phoenix Tapes* (1999), creative play reveals the psychic structures that lie under the surface of the superficially very different Hitchcock films which they assemble in a montage of clips. Müller explains his approach:

> While I collect and sort out the images an attitude towards the material starts developing. It expands from parasitic nesting in already existing visual material and the uncovering of hidden messages to dismantling and denunciation. I tear the image from its original context. . . . This strategy, comparable to associative and mercurial thinking, triggers a process of transformation.[14]

Müller and Giradet link scenes and dialogue about the mother in twenty of the films, organized in arbitrary dreamlike associations. "Why Don't You Love Me?" was made as independent art practice and occasionally shown in festivals, but invokes the equivalent process in practice-based research in an academic context. This practice can be seen as part of the lineage of the original "found footage genre," as defined broadly by Cecilia Hausheer and Christoph Settele in their 1992 compilation, which traces the work of pioneers such as Joseph Cornell, Bruce Connor, and Malcolm Le Grice in the pre-digital era.[15] Müller and Giradet's analysis is produced by the creative conjunction of sequences organized by a dream logic connecting shots by association: eye shots, phone calls, smoking cigarettes, and laughter. It irreversibly transforms the viewer's perception of this psychic dynamic within Hitchcock's cinema and lodges in the viewer's mind ready for future encounters with Hitchcock movies.

Double Take and Phoenix Tapes are part of an expanding presence of independent film in general inhabiting gallery spaces that has been established over the last thirty years. Installations and screenings take their place as part of a conceptual opening for a wider range of artistic practices that have come to inhabit a domain previously confined to traditional visual arts, such as painting and sculpture.[16] Painting itself has been repositioned as traditional approaches

Figure 2

are undermined, abandoning the subject, the object, and painting itself.[17] Godard's large scale exhibition *Voyage(s) en utopie* at the Pompidou Centre in 2006 and John Akomfrah's three screen *Vertigo Sea* (fig. 2) as part of the *Entangled Pasts 1768-now* exhibition at the Royal Academy in London are examples of prominent gallery exhibitions featuring films quoting fragments from diverse archival sources with an underlying analytical purpose. They provide a background context for the artists' working with Hitchcock.[18] It is familiarity with this changed gallery setting that enables Cousins's film, although it will be typically encountered in cinemas or on television, to intervene in a way which supplements but also displaces scholarly and critical commentary.

Cousins's film extends the experimental work that has taken place in the domain of the gallery into festivals and art house cinema. It is an approach that exemplifies a new and extended mode of criticism offering a model of uninhibited personal speculation that challenges some previous perceptions and reaches beyond the limits of written annotation. The formulas of academic writing generally efface their personal and subjective determinations.[19] Practice-based doctorates have become more common in universities and art colleges, and examples of experiments with Hitchcock, although created specifically for gallery and film festival exhibition, have become directly relevant to and have expanded the parameters of research in the institutions of higher education. The specificity of film is used in the creation of new knowledge, and its difference from and complementarity to traditional academic writing, with standard apparatus of footnotes and references, are understood and accepted.

Such work challenges the form and function of traditional research in the tertiary institutions of Anglophone education systems at this time, opening the highest level of formal academic degrees to unpredictable interactions between artwork and written text. This research has allowed artistic practice to inflect the concept of the Ph.D. degree, perhaps playing a role in the academy not unlike a Trojan horse entering the besieged city at night, opening ossified institutions to a whole range of new and genuinely interdisciplinary possibilities for research. Experimental work can combine theory and imaginative forms of thought in complex and changeable ways, and in their complexities they indicate the possibility of new versions of praxis. Many college courses encourage students (who will be familiar with musical and filmic "mashups") to use small-scale personal filmmaking as a means to develop their critical study of cinema, and the audiovisual essay is increasingly encouraged as a video equivalent of the written essay.[20] The extensions in the usage of pre-existent footage, fictional and factual, in online and social media digital play provides a new audio visual habitat for *My Name is Alfred Hitchcock*.

II

Mark Cousins initially made his name as a television producer and director providing intelligent insight into cinema with serious programs about films: *Scene by Scene* (1997-2003) examined the editing and detailed construction of individual sequences and scenes in conversation with their directors, a process applied posthumously to the analysis of Hitchcock sequences. He also introduced over sixty films for *Moviedrome*, a popular BBC series on cult films, in the 1990s. *The Story of Film: An Odyssey* (2011) was an epic fifteen-hour documentary series and book, extended with *The Story of Film: A New Generation* (2021). Cousins expanded the range of his address with a stylish poetic essay *I Am Belfast* (2015), on the city of his birth, and *March on Rome* (2022), about the rise of Fascism in Italy. He has continued to write and direct a prolific number of films exhibiting fresh and insightful ideas about cinema, in the last few years making feature-length essays with impact in festivals and cinemas, such as *The Eyes of Orson Welles* (2018), exploring Welles's previously unseen drawings and sketches. (There may even be an implicit duplication of Welles's dissembling in Cousins's Hitchcock film, which, like *F is For Fake*, begins by promising to tell only one lie).

My Name is Alfred Hitchcock was premiered in Telluride in September 2022 and subsequently shown in film festivals across Europe, Asia, and Latin America. It was released in Britain in the spring of 2023 against the backdrop of the formidable simultaneous opening of *Barbie* and *Oppenheimer* that followed shortly thereafter in the summer of that year. It is clearly positioned as an art house alternative, not a competitive feature. This formally innovative essay film gathers its material in six broad and poetic sections, titled 1. Escape, 2. Desire, 3. Loneliness, 4. Time, 5. Fulfilment, 6. Height. The third section best captures its tone throughout, offering a sympathetic if mischievous perspective and even occasionally poignant portrait of the director. Cousins has written that he thinks of *My Name is Alfred Hitchcock* "as a COVID film. . . . It's alert to loneliness and yearning for connection."[21]

A new version of Hitchcock's careful creation of his profile is an important context for the way in which Cousins structures his film. Giving Hitchcock two hours to talk in detail about what his films mean and how they work, the strategies in the documentary are to literally and figuratively restore Hitchcock's voice and partial image. Hitchcock critics and scholars are inevitably excluded and silenced here. Ironically, of course, the voice in the film is presented as both authentic and yet overtly ventriloquized, as the film's governing conceit "written and voiced by Alfred Hitchcock" is introduced and then undermined in the first few minutes: "I know I've been dead for forty years" says Alistair McGowan in his uncannily accurate Hitchcock voice—a kind of vocal celebrity waxwork. It is an indication of how Cousins's curiosity and questioning oscillates between respect and irreverence towards the established persona of Hitchcock

Figure 3

and his films. Cousins interposes his own imagery amongst the extracts of Hitchcock's films, opening with the exquisite swirls of a highly colored tropical fish and, near the end, the slowed turning of a red dress in movement. He includes stills (sometimes subtly animated) in the transition between sections. A haunting shot of a young woman in a gold top (wearing the same colors as Julie Andrews in *Torn Curtain* [1966]) who looks directly at the camera reappears several times, returning the spectator's stare (fig. 3). Its meaning is not immediately clear and Cousins explains "I made the film during lockdown, so I spent hours—days—looking through stock shots. This is an unusually impactful stock shot and represents exactly the sort of person we don't see in Hitch movies."[22]

The inventive montage of clips from Hitchcock is taken from a commendably broad and inclusive range of his output—the early English silent films through to the late American pictures, from *Downhill* (1927) and *The Farmer's Wife* (1928) to *Family Plot* (1976).[23] Occasionally the narration includes an intimate aside that directly addresses the present—for example, "What they call society can be terrible, can't it?" says "Hitchcock" rhetorically at one point while connecting the orange flashes caused by the camera bulb in *Rear Window* with atomic testing (fig. 4).

Challenging the digital world, juxtaposing the imperative of getting away from information overload and the compulsive

Figure 4

Figure 5

screentime spent on our mobile phones is contrasted with Tippi Hedren's relaxing pause for a cigarette by a children's playground in *The Birds* (1963): "You call this 'mindfulness' now, don't you."[24] These playful anachronisms, chronologically out of place, indicate different routes where Cousins brings Hitchcock to the present and transposes him to the contemporary world. The careful and conscious positioning of Hitchcock as a contemporary of ours, by such commentary as well as by including the sculpture by Antony Donaldson in Hackney, London (fig. 5), is a significant artistic decision, part of an assertion that while the film gives full expression to

Figure 6

Hitchcock's original views of his films, they also suggest critical views relevant to a contemporary world far beyond the one that historical films normally anticipate.

The documentary plays with hypotheses that are arguable and assertions that are untenable, sometimes deliberately: for example, the suggestion that in a moment of solitude walking outside in Los Angeles, Hitchcock came across and was so captivated by an exquisite image of berries touched by a trickle of water that he intentionally dropped the special cigarette lighter used in *Strangers on a Train* (1951) down a drain in order to hold the memory of this special moment is risible long before it is discarded as false at the end of the documentary. Unsurprisingly, with a running time of two hours, Cousins's film might have been stronger if tighter, shorter. The film's duration may relate to an artisanal (auteurial) production structure with a director's normal desire to "include almost everything," over-extending the running time without constraint.

Some of the details thrown into focus in the documentary replicate the inner satisfaction felt by the original viewers spotting one of the over forty cameo appearances Hitchcock made in his films. An epoch later, the professional cinephile or critic draws attention to other kinds of subtle details and hidden correspondences—often as proof of perspicacity and esoteric knowledge. Reviewers often display

Figure 7

and perform a softer version of the fetishised meticulosity of the "scholarly mode" in a disingenuous manner that is generally speculative. Cousins is similarly observant: speaking in the film, "Hitchcock" notes the use of precise color schemes and "the eagle eyed amongst you might have spotted . . . my homage to Paul Cezanne" in the carefully placed Cezanne paintings on the set of *Marnie* (fig. 6); and the film's commentary points out that "His geometry was not the world's geometry." Cousins's Hitchcock also refers to the knives on the wall in Sam's hardware store behind the private detective Arbogast in *Psycho* (fig. 7) and, less credibly, suggests that when we see "that bag of moss in the background—you know that Marion's car will be sunk in a mossy swamp."

These details raise questions of intentionality: Cezanne certainly, knives probably, but bags of fertilizer as a flashback and prolepsis for the car sinking in a mossy swamp, probably not. These are normally unnoticed and distracting signifiers on the sidelines of the text, and Cousins, like more than a few Hitchcock scholars, does not resist the lure of speculations, not all of which are persuasive. Conjecture about patterns of meaning are often proposed without awareness of production process or reference to audience reception.[25] More prudent critics and academic writers are careful and explicit about the status of the signifying elements they invoke, and cautiously and credibly address and answer such questions as: are they planted or unplanned? absorbed consciously or unconsciously? And, crucially, are they likely to be read by an audience? Like some of the sections in the Müller and Giradet tapes, Cousins certainly articulates the significance of subtle details and the presence of intricate subterranean patterns that feature in the films, and like most critical approaches assumes an aware and conscious intention by Hitchcock, whether or not he ever acknowledged it at the time. However, although they were raised a long time ago, the terms of the "death of the author" debate continue to question the grounds of many critical assertions and point towards the disingenuousness of many presuppositions. The debate raises underlying questions about the coherence of the subjectivity of the artist and the generative power of the subjectivity of the viewer, and aims to take some of these elements in unconscious meaning-making into clear and conscious analysis. *My Name is Alfred Hitchcock* balances the range of insights and propositions while playfully and reflexively undermining its own credibility.

Cousins's essay film does not touch on the serious denunciation of Hitchcock that Tippi Hedren made in 2009, an anticipation of #MeToo which grew to prominence several years later: "He suddenly grabbed me and put his hands on me. It was sexual, it was perverse and it was ugly."[26] Later a television film, *The Girl* (2012), explored the off-screen darkness in Hitchcock's psychology that seemed to be part of his relation with the actress while filming *The Birds* and *Marnie*. While it may be inappropriate for disputation about Hedren's claims to dominate discussion of the director, or indeed the actress, at this point in history it would be almost an implicit denial of serious allegations if they were effaced or erased. But Cousins made a conscious and clear decision:

> If the subject had been ignored, I would have found a way to deal with it. . . . Of course Hitchcock behaved disgracefully and she has been thoughtful and measured

in her accounting. But the tabloid response has been to allege that he did the same to other women. There are no other allegations that I'm aware of. On the contrary, Alfred Hitchcock's female collaborators often made a point of saying how simulating it was to work with him. I knew Janet Leigh and Teresa Wright and they both loved him. So did Ingrid Bergman. If his treatment of Tippi Hedren had been underreported, I'd have gone into it, but the tabloids and Donald Spoto seem to have ignored evidence and testimony from his many female collaborators. So I decided not to spread more rumours.[27]

The Hedren controversy relates also to the almost unexplored question of another kind of control—the cathartic power associated with Hitchcock's declared interest in "the means of telling the stories." In Cousins's account, the Hitchcock-voiced narration suggests "I love you my audience—I love playing with you." In response to the question from Penelope Houston, in one of his late interviews in *Sight and Sound*, "What is the deepest logic of your films?" Hitchcock summarized his film-making desire in uncompromising terms: "To put the audience through it."[28] The issue of the filmmaker's creation of (and spectators' connivance with) desire for purgative emotional manipulation is articulated by Jean-Luc Godard in metaphoric form as part of his eight-hour experimental essay *Histoire(s) du Cinéma, (Chapter Four (a) The Control of the Universe)*:

Alfred Hitchcock succeeded
where Alexander, Julius Caesar, Hitler and Napoleon
had all failed
by taking control of the universe.
Perhaps there are less than ten thousand people
who haven't forgotten Cézanne's apple
but there must be a billion spectators
who will remember the lighter
 the stranger on the train[29]

Godard's critique of mainstream fictional narratives and the cathartic effects they deliver through a signifying system that effaces itself is manifest in his use of an extract from an interview with Hitchcock:

> We have a rectangular screen in a movie house
> And this rectangular screen has got to be filled
> with a succession of images
> that's where the ideas come from
> one picture comes up after another
> the public aren't aware of what we call montage
> or in other words the cutting of one image to another
> they go by so rapidly that they are absorbed by
>   the content
> that they look at on the screen

In his film Godard describes Hitchcock as the "greatest creator of forms" and connects this with history and politics, ancient and modern, locating the exercise of power in the mechanism in the sign: "It is forms that tell us finally what lies at the bottom of things." It is the politics of representation where the control of our universe takes place.

There are echoes of Godard's politics of form in different parts of Cousins's documentary. Perhaps the most memorable and persuasive of these is the suggestion that Hitchcock used extended, uncut shots to reinforce the reality of the concentration camp footage he worked on with Sidney Bernstein, footage indelibly illustrating, as "that gentleman after my own heart John Buchan said, there's just a thin protection to civilisation." Cousins raises questions normally discussed in seminar rooms, conferences, and in specialist journals. The significant achievement of *My Name is Alfred Hitchcock* is that it opens the work of the films and, compared with standard critical and academic discourse, reaches a significantly wider audience in a more imaginative and playful way.

Notes

1. Interestingly, audio compression on streaming services mean that audio quality on films that are streamed is much worse than cinema or television broadcast quality, and it is significant that 40% of people on Netflix use same language subtitles. See https://www.theguardian.com/tv-and-radio/2023/jan/28/mumbling-actors-bad-speakers-or-lazy-listeners-why-everyone-is-watching-tv-with-subtitles-on.

2. For a detailed history of the impact of French theory on the development of film studies in Britain, see Colm McAuliffe, *Film, In Theory: How the BFI Transformed Film Culture* (London: Bloomsbury, forthcoming 2024).

3. Andrew Sarris, *The American Cinema* (New York: E.P. Dutton, 1968).

4. Inquiring for a joint exhibition combining the material in the University of Galway Archive and the MPAA in 2010, they welcomed the prospect of an exhibition about John Huston: "Thank god for that. Hitchcock is the only director they ever seem to want."

5. "The spectator brings the work in contact with the external world by deciphering and interpreting its inner qualification." Quoted in Marcel Duchamp, "The Creative Act," in Calvin Tomkins, *DUCHAMP A Biography* (London: Pimlico, 1996), 509-10, online at https://sites.evergreen.edu/politicalshakespeares/wp-content/uploads/sites/226/2015/12/Duchamp-The-Creative-Act.pdf.

6. Roland Barthes, "The Death of the Author," in *The Rustle of Language* (Berkeley and Los Angeles: University of California Press, 1989), 50.

7. Werner Herzog offers hypothetical speculations about the painters of the walls of the Chauvet cave in *Cave of Forgotten Dreams* (2010).

8. Anna Della Subin, "Wreckage of Ellipses," *London Review of Books* 46, no. 3 (February 2024); online at https://www.lrb.co.uk/the-paper/v46/n03/anna-della-subin/wreckage-of-ellipses.

9. Kim Simpson's work on anonymous eighteenth century "amatory fiction" makes it clear that interpretation changes when gender is assumed as male or female in an anonymous text. See Kim Simpson, "The 'Little Arts' of Amatory Fiction: Identity, Performance and Process" (Ph.D. thesis, University of Kent at Canterbury, 2014); online at https://kar.kent.ac.uk/48720/1/145Kim%20Simpson%20The%20Little%20Arts%20of%20Amatory%20Fiction.pdf.

10. André Bazin, "Hitchcock vs. Hitchcock," in *Focus on Hitchcock*, ed. Albert J. LaValley (Englewood, NJ: Prentice-Hall, 1972), 64.

11. François Truffaut, with the collaboration of Helen G. Scott, *Hitchcock* (London: Secker & Warburg, 1966).

12. For extended discussions of Hitchcock in art cinema, see Bernard McCarron, *The Paradigm Case: The Cinema of Hitchcock and the Contemporary Visual Arts* (Oxford: Peter Lang, 2015); and Christine Sprengler, *Hitchcock and Contemporary Art* (London: Palgrave, 2014).

13. See http://www.johangrimonprez.be/main/Film_DoubleTake_Synopsis.html.

14. Matthias Müller, "Statement," in Cecilia Hausheer and Christoph Settele, eds., *Found Footage Film* (Lucerne: VIPER, 1992), 117.

15. In a later era this term has also been applied to a subgenre of horror films such as *The Blair Witch Project, Cloverfield, Paranormal Activity*, and *Cannibal Holocaust* that uses *faux-vérité* footage "discovered" by survivors.

16. Discussed in Rod Stoneman, "The Installation of the Exotic," *KINEMA: A Journal for Film and Audiovisual Media* (Spring 2015), online at https://doi.org/10.15353/kinema.vi.1322.

17. See Roland Barthes, *Sollers* (London: Athlone Press, 1987), 72.

18. *Voyage(s) en utopie / Travel(s) in Utopia, JLG, 1946-2006, In Search of Lost Theorem*, May 11–August 14, 2006, Pompidou Centre, Paris; *Entangled Pasts, 1768-now: Art, Colonialism and Change*, February 3–April 28, 2024, Royal Academy, London.

19. Roland Barthes's focus on the disparity between the third person of "histoire" and first person of "discours" is the key distinction here; see "The Discourse of History," in *The Rustle of Language* (Berkeley and Los Angeles: University of California Press, 1989), 127-40.

20. Videographic film studies are discussed by Catherine Grant in "How Long is a Piece of String: On the Practice, Scope, and Value of Videographic Film Studies and Criticism," *REFRAME*, online at reframe.sussex.ac.uk/audiovisualessay/frankfurt-papers/catherine-grant/.

21. Email to the author, March 11, 2024.

22. Email to the author, March 11, 2024.

23. Cousins's film deploys every Hitchcock film with the exception of *Secret Agent* (1936). He told me that "I had *Secret Agent* in, but then cut it out. I didn't on purpose try to cover everything—

I was just looking for a kind of aesthetic or social electricity" (email to the author, March 11, 2024).

24. For an extensive polemical critique of the digital world, see Jonathan Crary's *Scorched Earth* (London: Verso, 2022).

25. For example, perambulation, street crossing, and jaywalking in *I Confess* would not have been noticed by spectators then or now, and are unlikely to have been part of Hitchcock's conscious patterning. They have, however, attracted academic interest, indicated in John Bruns's paper "The Jaywalking Priest: Going Off the Grid in Hitchcock's *I Confess*," presented at the Hitchcock International Symposium at University College, London, September 7-8, 2023.

26. Quoted in Alan Evans, "Tippi Hedren: Alfred Hitchcock Sexually Assaulted Me," *The Guardian*, October 31, 2016, online at https://www.theguardian.com/film/2016/oct/31/tippi-hedren-alfred-hitchcock-sexually-assaulted-me.

27. Email to the author, April 2, 2024.

28. Penelope Houston, "The Figure in the Carpet," *Sight and Sound* 32 no. 4 (Autumn 1963): 160.

29. To reproduce the Godard and Hitchcock interview sections of voice-over in print, I have followed the format in Volume 4 of the books of *Histoire(s)* produced to accompany the soundtracks on CD (Munich: ECM Records, 1999), 43.

Contributors

Elisabeth Karlin is a playwright in New York. Her plays have won several awards and have been produced in New York and Los Angeles. Her work is published by Next Stage Press and Smith and Kraus Publishers. She also writes about film whenever the opportunity arises. She has been a frequent contributor to the Alfred Hitchcock Geek blog, covering a wide range of subjects. Her essay "Beyond the Blonde: The Dynamic Heroines of Hitchcock" appeared in the *Hitchcock Annual* 25.

Amy Lawrence is Professor Emerita at Dartmouth College. She has written on several Hitchcock films: *Blackmail* and *Notorious* (in *Echo and Narcissus: Women's Voices in Classical Hollywood Cinema*, 1991), *Rope* ("American Shame," in *Hitchcock's America*, edited by Jonathan Freedman and Rick Millington, 1999), and *I Confess* (in *The Passion of Montgomery Clift*, 2010).

Thomas Leitch, the Unidel Andrew B. Kirkpatrick Chair in Writing at the University of Delaware, is the author of *Find the Director and Other Hitchcock Games* and *The Encyclopedia of Alfred Hitchcock*, and the coeditor, with Leland Poague, of *A Companion to Alfred Hitchcock*. His most recent book is the edited collection *The Scandal of Adaptation*.

Subarna Mondal is an Assistant Professor of English at The Sanskrit College and University, Kolkata, India. She holds a Ph.D. from Jadavpur University, Department of Film Studies. Her areas of interest include late-Victorian Gothic literature, the Gothic on screen, Animal Studies, and the films of Alfred Hitchcock. Her articles have appeared in *Northern Lights: Film and Media Studies Yearbook*, *Humanities*, and edited collections published by Palgrave Macmillan and Manchester University

Press. Her book *Alfred Hitchcock's Psycho and Taxidermy: Fashioning Corpses* was published by Bloomsbury Academic in February 2024.

David Sterritt is a film professor at the Maryland Institute College of Art and past chair of the New York Film Critics Circle and the National Society of Film Critics. He was film critic of *The Christian Science Monitor* for decades, has lectured on Hitchcock at the National Gallery of Art, the Brooklyn Museum, the Motion Picture Association of America, and elsewhere, and has written and edited fifteen books, two of them on Hitchcock.

Rod Stoneman is an Emeritus Professor at the University of Galway. He was a Deputy Commissioning Editor in the Independent Film and Video Department at Channel 4 Television from 1983-93, Chief Executive of Bord Scannán na hÉireann/The Irish Film Board from 1993-2003, and the Director of the Huston School of Film & Digital Media from 2003-15. He has made a number of documentaries, including *Ireland: The Silent Voices, Italy: The Image Business*, and *Between Object and Image*. He is the author of *Chávez: The Revolution Will Not Be Televised, Seeing is Believing: The Politics of the Visual*, and (with Duncan Petrie) *Educating Filmmakers*.

Garrett A. Sullivan, Jr., is Edwin Erle Sparks Professor of English at Penn State University. His most recent books are *Shakespeare and British World War Two Film* (Cambridge, 2022) and, with Greg Semenza, *Powell and Pressburger's War: The Art of Propaganda, 1939-1946* (Bloomsbury, 2023).